SOCIAL CONFLICTS
IN THE ROMAN REPUBLIC

ANCIENT CULTURE AND SOCIETY

General Editor
M. I. FINLEY

Professor of Ancient History,
University of Cambridge

SOCIAL CONFLICTS
IN THE
ROMAN REPUBLIC

P. A. BRUNT

Camden Professor of Ancient History
at the University of Oxford

W · W · NORTON & COMPANY · INC · *NEW YORK*

CONTENTS

PREFACE

This little book is not a general history of the internal affairs of Rome in the Republic. Its subject is defined by the title; it is concerned with the conflicts that arose between orders and classes in society. It thus has little on the factions that divided the ruling class itself, which in my view were less coherent and lasting and far more difficult to identify than is now commonly supposed, and only so much is said of the ambitions and manoeuvres of powerful individuals—the importance of which I do not dispute—as is necessary to follow the course of the social conflicts. I have begun by sketching the effects of Rome's expansion on the internal structure of the state and the general economic conditions prevalent in ancient Italy; the development of the political framework, including the working of *clientelae* and the character of the nobility as well as constitutional principles and changes, is delineated chronologically in the chapters that follow. The student of the late Republic should perhaps be warned that the last three chapters are meant to be read in the light of all that preceded them.

I am much indebted for helpful criticisms to Professor M. I. Finley, the general editor of this series, and to Dr. J. M. Moore of Radley College, who read the text in typescript. The views expressed and any remaining errors are my own.

P. A. BRUNT

CHRONOLOGICAL TABLE

Dates before 300 are traditional and only approximate.

BC

754	Rome founded.
509	Republic established.
494	Tribunate of the plebs created.
451–0	Decemvirs codify laws (Twelve Tables).
396	Conquest of Veii.
390	Gauls sack Rome.
366	First plebeian consul.
338	Many Latin cities, and Capua, become Roman.
287	Hortensian law (end of strife of patricians and plebeians).
280–75	War with Pyrrhus; at its end Roman control of Italy (except Cisalpine Gaul) virtually complete.
264–41	First war with Carthage.
241, 227	Roman provinces constituted in Sicily and Sardinia.
c. 225–170	Conquest of Cisalpine Gaul.
218–201	Second war with Carthage (Hannibal's invasion).
c. 200	Provinces formed in Spain ·(not fully pacified till 19).
200–146	Intermittent wars in east leading to annexation of Macedon and part of Greece.
154–133	Serious wars in Spain.
149–146	Third war with Carthage, leading to annexation of part of North Africa.
133	Tiberius Gracchus tribune.
129	Province of 'Asia' (in western Asia Minor) formed.
125–121	Conquests in South France (later the province of Transalpine Gaul).
123–121	Tribunates and death of Gaius Gracchus.
112–106	Jugurthine war (Marius' first consulship, 107).

CHRONOLOGICAL TABLE

113–101	Cimbric war.
103, 100	Saturninus' tribunates.
91	Drusus' tribunate. Outbreak of Social war.
90–81	Enfranchisement of Italy.
88–84	War with Mithridates.
88	Sulla's first march on Rome.
87–6, 83–1	Civil wars.
82	Sullan autocracy and legislation.
80–72	Sertorian war in Spain.
78–77	Lepidus' rising in Italy.
74	Outbreak of Mithridatic war in East.
73–71	Slave revolt in Italy.
70	Pompey and Crassus consuls.
67–62	Pompey's pirate and eastern campaigns, and annexations.
63	Cicero consul. Catiline's conspiracy.
59	Caesar's first consulship. First triumvirate.
58	Clodius tribune.
58–50	Caesar conquers rest of Transalpine Gaul.
52	Clodius murdered.
49–45	Civil wars between Caesar and Pompeians.
44	Caesar killed.
44–42	Civil wars between Caesarians and Republicans.
43	Second Triumvirate formed.
43–36	Sextus Pompey controls Sicily and the seas.
32—0	Civil war between Octavian and Antony.
30	Octavian in supreme control. Egypt annexed.
27	Octavian becomes Augustus. Beginning of the Principate.

A NOTE ON COINS AND MEASURES

The early Romans used cattle as a measure of value (*pecunia*, money, comes from *pecus*, herd), bronze by weight for purposes of exchanges. The earliest coins were also of bronze. Silver and gold were first minted in the third century. For the last 200 years covered in this book the standard coin was the silver *denarius*, weighing about 60 grains; I give all money figures in *denarii*. (A *denarius* was worth 4 sesterces.) It is misleading to give a modern monetary equivalent based on its weight and purity; what matters is what the *denarius* would buy. This too cannot be precisely stated, but some idea of its value is given on p. 14.

The unit of land measurement was the *iugerum*, about two-thirds of an acre.

ANCIENT CULTURE AND SOCIETY

SOCIAL CONFLICTS
IN THE ROMAN REPUBLIC

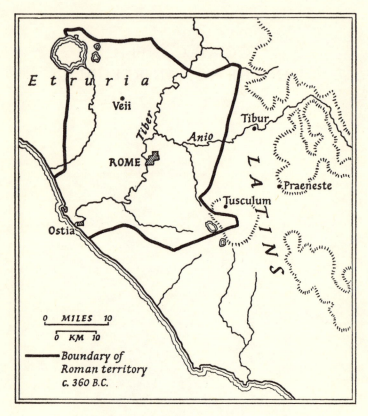

Etruria

Veii

Tiber

Anio

Tibur

ROME

LATINS

Tusculum

Praeneste

Ostia

0 MILES 10

0 KM 10

Boundary of
Roman territory
c. 360 B.C.

1. Early Rome and Her Neighbours c. 360 B.C.

The Background, Roman Expansion and Its Results

ACCORDING to tradition, the Romans expelled the Etruscan king, Tarquin the Proud, and established a republic in 509[1]; the date has been challenged, but in my view it is roughly correct. The Republic was overthrown in the last century before Christ. It is impossible to set this change in any particular year. Republican institution sceased to work normally in 59 as a result of the combination between Pompey and Julius Caesar, who dominated the state for a decade; their quarrel led to civil wars, briefly interrupted by the despotism of Caesar and soon renewed after his assassination; eventually his adopted son and heir, Caesar Augustus, emerged as the victor and founded the system of barely veiled monarchy which we call the Principate. The revolution was complete at least by the memorable day, 13 January 27, when the master of the armies gave out that he had restored the ancient Republic. So this book covers almost five centuries.

In 509 Roman territory comprised only some 800 square kilometres. The walled city was itself ever in danger of foreign attack. Meetings of the people could be suspended if a flag was run up on the Janiculum, the hill just across the Tiber, to denote that an Etruscan raiding force was in sight. The Romans could as yet field no more than two legions, some 8,000 men.

By 27 the whole of Italy was Roman, and all its free inhabitants, except for foreign immigrants and some Alpine tribes, were citizens; hundreds of thousands of citizens also lived in provinces overseas. In 28 Augustus' census enumerated just over four millions; in my judgement women and children over the age of one, as well as adult males (over seventeen) were included, but the returns are unlikely to have been complete, and a true total might well have been five millions. (Republican

[1] All dates are BC, unless otherwise stated.

census returns were certainly restricted to males over seventeen, and figures based on these returns will be reported later.) Roman dominion now extended from the Channel to the Sahara and from the Straits of Gibraltar to the Euphrates; most of this area was already under Roman control by 146 (not Gaul or the interior of Asia Minor), though less was then under direct Roman administration; even in 27 principalities and republics on the borders or even within the confines of the empire preserved a degree of independence as 'client' states. Augustus, however, considered these 'client' states to be parts of the empire, and they were no less under Roman control than the subjects, who were also allowed much local autonomy. Over most of Italy Roman suzerainty went back to about 280. So early had Rome outstripped the natural proportions of a city state, yet she retained the institutions of such a state until the fall of the Republic.

Roman expansion was of course the result of foreign wars, which did not cease even amid the grave internal strife which began in 133. Of all aspects of Republican history it is the most important, if only because it was the precondition of that lasting dissemination of Graeco-Roman culture which the 'immense majesty of the Roman peace' promoted. Though not the subject of this book, it forms its essential background. War and conquest transformed the economy of Italy, and helped at first to resolve, later to exacerbate social conflict. Internal struggles and foreign wars were often entangled, and reacted on each other. Expansion in itself distorted the working of political institutions, the machinery would-be social reformers had to use. It even changed the very meaning of the term 'Romans'.

The early Romans, though they probably comprised men of Sabine and Etruscan origin, were all Latins by speech and were normally allies or members of a league embracing all the other neighbouring Latin cities. Rome acquired dominance over this league, and after the Latins had tried in vain to shake off her control, dissolved the league and made many of its members citizens (338). About the same time the Capuans, who spoke Oscan, a

2

language at least as different from Latin as French from Italian, were also enfranchised, and thus lost their independence. This practice of enfranchising other Italian peoples was frequently pursued down to the middle of the third century. All the new citizens were bound, like the old, to pay taxes and fight in Rome's armies, and all had the same rights of intermarriage and private contractual relations, but many, like the Capuans, were initially denied the right to vote or hold office at Rome; they preserved some local self-government. This inferiority was resented by the Capuans, who revolted in 216; by a process we can hardly trace, which was probably complete before 90, it was removed, and all received full rights. We happen to know that Volscian Arpinum, once Oscan in speech, was upgraded in this way in 188; it was the birthplace of Marius, who saved Rome from the German menace in 102–101, and of Cicero. Marius was only a second or third generation Roman with full rights. This liberality with the citizenship, though peculiar to Rome, is easily intelligible; it helped to give Rome numerical superiority over each successive enemy, and was an important factor in the growth of her strength.

It is less clear why Rome, unlike other ancient states, also allowed slaves manumitted by citizens to acquire citizenship along with freedom. These freedmen were not permitted to serve in the army, save in rare crises, though they could be enlisted to row in the fleets. Still, their descendants, born in freedom, were not subject to any disability and added to Rome's numerical strength. As time went on, the influx of slaves from outside Italy and the number of manumissions vastly increased, and a high, though unknown, proportion of citizens by Augustus' time had servile and foreign blood in their veins.

Roman numbers grew in another way. The small and not very fertile territory the city held in 509 could not long have supported an expanding population. Annexations alone could provide additional subsistence for new, hungry mouths. In 396 Rome conquered Veii north of the Tiber and distributed the land among her own citizens; her territory increased by more than a third. Veii disappeared

3

as an independent state. Rome did not usually proceed with such severity, but it was common for her (we are told) to take a third of the land of Italian peoples she conquered, and from time to time part of this land was divided among poor Romans. Thus landless citizens, such as younger sons, could establish households of their own, increase and multiply.

By the time of Hannibal's invasion of Italy in 218 Roman territory (as distinct from that of her subject allies) already amounted to some 25,000 square kilometres and registered Roman citizens (males over seventeen) numbered at least 270,000. Many of her allies went over to Hannibal, and were punished by further sequestrations; moreover, in the early second century great stretches of land were annexed from Gauls and Ligurians in north Italy. We cannot determine the precise extent of Roman territory in this period, but the census figures, which were probably increasingly incomplete, suggest that in the second century the number of adult male citizens rose well above 400,000.

For long Rome's strength had not depended only on the number of Romans. Other Italian peoples were bound to her in perpetual alliances. They retained their local autonomy, and paid no tribute to Rome, but were obliged to find contingents for Rome's armies at their own cost and to fight in wars that were not of their own choosing; in return, they enjoyed Roman protection. By the middle of the third century this network of alliances extended over the whole of peninsular Italy south of a line running roughly from Pisa to Rimini. In 225 the allies numbered about 600,000. The country to the north, populated by Ligurians, Gauls and Veneti, was known in the Republic after the most powerful of its inhabitants as Cisalpine Gaul; it was conquered between 225 and about 170, though the pacification of the wilder mountainous areas was more protracted.

Among the allies the Latin cities occupied a special place. After incorporating most of the old Latin communities in her own citizen body in 338, Rome continued to found new 'Latin' colonies in strategic sites all over Italy;

4

the last were established early in the second century in Cisalpine Gaul. Most of the settlers were Romans who forfeited their citizenship at Rome in return for land and for membership of new communities with local self-government. The colonies were generally too distant from Rome for political rights there to have seemed of much value at the time; however, most and probably all Latins were entitled to inherit and own land in Roman territory and to intermarry with Romans in such a way that the children took the status of the father. From the late second century those who obtained local magistracies automatically became Roman citizens; in this way the local ruling class were more closely bound to the suzerain. Subject to certain conditions indeed any Latin could obtain Roman citizenship merely by migrating to Roman territory. These privileges, coupled with their memory of Roman descent and often perhaps with the fact that they were on bad terms with surrounding peoples, whose land had been confiscated for their benefit and whom they were designed to keep in check, no doubt explain why with few exceptions the Latin colonies were loyal to Rome in every crisis.

That was not true of all the other allies. Most of them spoke languages unintelligible to Latins (the Etruscan tongue was not even Indo-European) and most had been brought by force under Roman hegemony. For generations they were restive at their subjection. After Hannibal's defeat they had no further chance of obtaining foreign aid to assert their independence. Rome's power seemed irresistible. Moreover for the next century peninsular Italy enjoyed internal peace, undisturbed and unexampled. Roman and Latin settlers, scattered throughout the land, spread Roman ideas and the Latin language; remote allied towns might remodel their institutions on the Roman pattern. In the meantime Rome was acquiring her empire in the Mediterranean, partly by the valour of allied soldiers; between half and two-thirds of her armies were composed of Latins and other allies. But though the Italians contributed heavily to Rome's victories, they had a far smaller share in the profits of empire, and none of the dignity and honour that accrued from imperial power; indeed, they were themselves occasionally subjected to arbitrary interferences in their own affairs from Rome, and their persons were not protected against the most capricious Roman commanders. A demand arose among the allies that they should be granted equality of status by the extension of the Roman franchise. It was rejected and most of them revolted in 90. Even then their object was not to recover their old independence but to set up a new federal state, called Italia, which in many ways was modelled on the Roman.

This 'Social' war (the war against the *socii* or allies) was one of the most bloody Rome ever fought, and the most futile. Rome could only subdue the rebels by buying off the Latins and other loyal allies with the very grant of citizenship she had previously refused. Moreover the struggle set in train a series of events which led to further wars among the citizens themselves (87–86, 83–81); the rival factions at Rome in their search for support had to concede the franchise even to the former rebels. Hence, all the peoples of *peninsular* Italy became Romans. In 69 an incomplete census revealed 910,000 adult male citizens; a more accurate count might well have given about 1,200,000. The people of Cisalpine Gaul, apart from Roman and former Latin settlers there, only received Latin rights, but after a prolonged agitation they too were enfranchised by Caesar in 49. The whole Italian mainland was thus Roman in the full sense; only provincials were subjects.

Clearly no account of Roman social conflicts in the Republic can be confined to those which solely or primarily affected only the city of Rome and its inhabitants. Even in the time of Caesar and Augustus, when the urban population was enormously swollen, it is unlikely that more than 15% of Roman citizens of all ages and both sexes lived in the city itself. Rome was indeed the arena in which all political decisions had to be taken by law, and these decisions were often influenced or determined by the wishes or interests of its inhabitants, sometimes by riots which fill a large place in the annals of the late Republic.

6

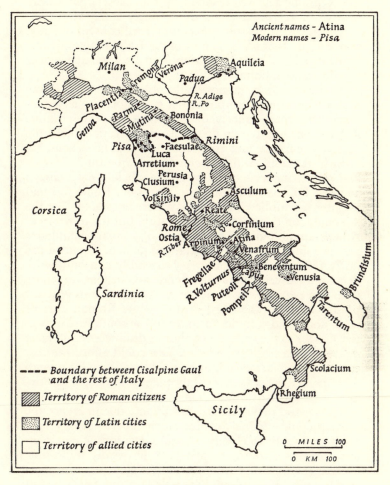

2. Italy in 133 B.C.

But in the last resort the course of the revolution in which the Republic fell was decided by the soldiers, who were nearly all recruited from the country folk. Moreover, Augustus based his rule on the universal consent of Italy, above all on that of the gentry of the Italian towns. Rome had turned Italy into a nation, and he appeared as the champion of national traditions.

By transcending the normal limits of a city state Rome denied herself the very possibility of democracy, as democracy was then conceived. The idea of representative government had barely arisen. In democratic Athens the ordinary citizens met frequently in popular assemblies open to them all, which decided every question of policy and closely supervised the executive officials; each citizen counted for one and not more than one. Rome too had popular assemblies, though they were not based, like the Athenian, on the principle of equality. But the territory of Athens amounted to only some 2,650 square kilometres and her citizens numbered perhaps 50,000. Toynbee has justly remarked that a primary assembly can only work democratically, if voters can attend without spending more than two nights away from home. At Athens this was just possible; but by the third century some Roman citizens were domiciled a hundred miles to the south and almost twice as far to the east. Much shorter distances would have deterred men from attendance. Few could afford the cost of travel. The farmer might be unable to leave his plough for a day. In order that rural dwellers might not theoretically be at a disadvantage, long notice had to be given of meetings, and they were necessarily infrequent. Hence the citizens could neither acquire much experience of affairs nor supervise them closely, nor take decisions in emergencies. Moreover, it must have been physically impossible even in the fourth century for more than a small proportion to meet in one place, hear a debate and vote. Only at the very end of the Republic was provision made for 70,000 to vote together, about 6% of the total citizen body. Even if the assemblies had been in principle democratically constituted, they could not have worked democratically and fairly. In fact the 'centuriate' assembly,

8

which elected the chief magistrates, was not democratic at all, but it may well have been representative of the rich, who controlled it, wherever they were domiciled, as they could afford to visit Rome for the annual elections. Ostensibly more democratic, the 'tribal' assembly was ultimately dominated by those who lived in or near the city. But the real power always belonged to the aristocratic Senate, which could normally manipulate and check the assemblies, and in a state as large as Rome became early in its history, there was no sensible alternative to oligarchy, given the absence of representative democratic institutions, except the rule of one man.

The Romans themselves contrasted favourably their liberality in granting citizenship with the exclusiveness of Athens. It is perfectly true that their liberality gradually did much to win the loyalty of subjects first in Italy and later, from Caesar's time, in the provinces. This policy could only have succeeded because the Roman system was undemocratic. If most decisions had rested with truly democratic assemblies, the franchise would have meant little to distant Apulians or Sabines or Umbrians. In the aristocratic Roman system, however, the local nobility of the Italian towns had some prospect of admittance to the ruling class at Rome, once they had obtained the citizenship. A generation or two from the enfranchisement of Tusculum its leading citizen, Lucius Fulvius, became consul (322) and founded one of the first families at Rome.

The Italian allies, and indeed the municipalities of Roman citizens scattered over Italy, were governed domestically in much the same way as the Romans. They had their own popular assemblies, their own elected magistrates, their own councils of men of birth and wealth, sitting for life. No doubt in these small communities, of which we know little, there were lively internal struggles, feuds between families that could result in bloodshed when the Roman state was itself torn by civil wars, and political disputes dividing classes; at Arpinum in the late second century Cicero's grandfather opposed a ballot law advocated by a kinsman of Marius, and modelled on those which popular tribunes had passed at Rome. In general the local governments were oligarchic, and Rome could be counted on to suppress any movements disruptive of the established order; for instance, in 265 Rome helped the lords of Volsinii to put down a servile revolution. The local nobilities, therefore, dominated their home towns. It was they who made known to the Senate the wishes of their people, which were their own wishes, and they could exercise influence through ties of friendship and hospitality which bound them to the great houses of Rome. For a long time the allied leaders were attached to maintaining the separate identity of their communes. In 215 well-to-do Praenestines who served on horse refused an offer of Roman citizenship. But in 90 it was the leading men who demanded Italian enfranchisement.

No doubt they wanted equal rank for its own sake. But it was now also clear that as citizens they would not forfeit local control and that they would acquire greater influence in the centre. Arpinum, whose people enjoyed the citizenship, had no less self-government at home than the allies who lacked it. But the Arpinates could also vote at Rome, and as votes were seldom given for nothing, they could expect favours of all kinds, even gifts of money. The suffrages of the local ruling classes, men who could come to Rome for the elections, would count heavily in the centuriate assembly. Moreover, the career of Marius, who had been six times consul, and perhaps of other *parvenus* who had recently risen to high office at Rome and may also have been of municipal origin, may have suggested that in course of time the allied magnates too might attain great dignity in Rome. Such hopes were fulfilled. After the enfranchisement of Italy candidates for higher Roman magistracies needed to woo support among the upper class in the most distant towns. Cicero, for instance, planned to canvass in Cisalpine Gaul; no region was more remote, and most of the towns there had only the Latin right, which meant that a mere handful of their inhabitants, the ex-magistrates, possessed the suffrage; but they were necessarily rich, and their votes were worth soliciting. Minor offices at Rome were filled by the tribal assembly, in which rich voters did not preponderate, but local magnates had a better chance of securing these for themselves, if they could, perhaps at their own cost, turn out the people of their own and neighbouring municipalities to vote for a 'favourite son'. Thus Gnaeus Plancius was elected aedile for 54 because virtually the whole population of his home town, Atina, and of the surrounding towns travelled a hundred miles to support him.

As time went on, the Italian *noblesse* rose higher. The soldier, orator and historian Gaius Asinius Pollio was consul in 40, when Virgil dedicated to him his fourth eclogue; he was apparently a grandson of a rebel leader of 90, Herius Asinius. By that time the Senate was packed with 'municipal' figures. Wars and proscriptions hastened the diminution of the old Roman nobility; their places were taken by 'all the flower of the towns in every part of Italy', 'the good, substantial men' whom (according to Claudius) Augustus and Tiberius wished to see in the Senate. To Catiline, the scion of a decayed patrician house, the Arpinate Cicero was still an 'outsider' (*inquilinus*), but the future lay with the Ciceros, not the Catilines.

Much of this book will be concerned with social conflicts between the rich and poor. But contests for privilege and dignity among the upper class were not less important and interacted on this class struggle, and none of these contests was more severe or profound in its effects than that which has just been sketched.

The earliest such contest was between the patricians and the rich plebeians (Chapter 3). The latter at last secured an equal right to office with the backing of the poor citizens, whose claims to relief from social misery they intermittently championed. However, this misery was probably alleviated chiefly by annexations of enemy territory and distributions of land to the poor. In this early period expansion seems to have mitigated social tensions. Not that they were altogether removed, or that anything resembling economic equality was ever achieved at Rome. Service in the legions was normally restricted to citizens who could equip themselves with weapons and defensive armour; there was a property qualification, and those who possessed it were called *assidui*, i.e. men who were

3. Italy: Physical Features

permanently settled on their own piece of land; the rest were *proletarii*, whose service to the state consisted in the offspring (*proles*) they raised, or *capite censi*, men who were counted by heads, having no property to speak of. In crises even *proletarii* were called up and armed at the public cost, for instance in the Hannibalic war. In my view they were then already a majority of the citizens. If popular agitation at Rome almost ceased for a hundred and fifty years after 287, the reason may partly be that there were few potential leaders for the masses, once the aspirations of the richer plebeians for office had been satisfied. But expansion had probably at least diminished the extent of social discontent. In 264 the people voted to interfere in Sicily against the will of the Senate and thus provoked a long and arduous struggle with Carthage ending only in 241; they hoped to grow rich on booty. By contrast, in 200 the Senate had to inveigle a war-weary people into approving hostilities with Macedon.

Between these two events there had been fearful loss of life and severe taxation in the prolonged struggle with Carthage. In the second war (218–201) half the men between eighteen and forty-six qualified for legionary service were generally under arms, many for several years at a stretch; the average was seven. Soldiers who campaigned in Spain, Sicily or Greece, could not even visit their homes on winter leave. Victory over Carthage did not bring settled peace. Cisalpine Gaul had to be subdued; there were several expeditions to Greece or Asia; the pacification of Spain had only begun—it was not completed until 19; two and often four legions were stationed there. On average the Romans had on paper 47,000 citizens in the field each year from 200 to 168, and not many fewer thereafter. If we add Italians with the armies and fleets, the nominal average rises to 130,000, and even if many units were not at full strength, it can hardly be much below 110,000.

As a rule the citizens who bore this burden were the *assidui*. They numbered only about 100,000 in the Hannibalic war. Not only were *proletarii* then enlisted, but the property qualification was permanently reduced. In the

SOCIAL CONFLICTS IN ROMAN REPUBLIC

second century it sank again to 400 *denarii*. On an estimate, made about AD 60, that sum would have purchased little more than an acre of cultivable land not under vines, far too little for subsistence (Columella III, 3, 8). Land values in the second century are unknown, but it seems unlikely that even then 400 *denarii* can have represented the value of more than a cottage, garden and some personal belongings. Cicero reckoned that a skilled slave could earn three quarters of a *denarius* a day, not necessarily every day in the year (*For Roscius the Comedian* 28). The soldier himself received 120 a year, from which the state normally deducted the cost of food, clothes and arms; it is significant that it could no longer expect him to equip himself. This must have been a living wage, perhaps not much more; after Caesar had raised it to 225, it was still regarded as meagre, as mutinies in AD 14 showed. Yet the property qualification for a second century legionary was only three and a third times his wage.

Occasionally soldiers received rich booty, and we hear of volunteers who were attracted by this prospect or by a life of adventure. But exemption from service was a treasured privilege, and on ten occasions between 193 and 130 we hear of difficulties, sometimes of outright resistance, in the levy of troops or their retention under the standards. In 133 Tiberius Gracchus and others expressed fears of depopulation; yet there were more adult males registered than in 218, and their fears make no sense unless they knew of a decline in the number of *assidui*. Boys below the military age were now conscripted. To mitigate hardship, an effort had already been made to keep soldiers in Spain no more than six years. The maximum number of campaigns that could be required, twenty in Polybius' time, was apparently reduced before 108 by laws which then had to be repealed. In the following year the Senate could assume that Marius' popularity would vanish if he had to conscribe *assidui*, to reinforce two legions in Africa, though he cannot have needed more than 5,000 Roman recruits; only 40,000 citizens were then under arms, and perhaps twice as many allies.

Marius escaped from his dilemma by enlisting *proletarii*

14

as volunteers; they expected booty and were not disappointed. The property qualification was never enforced again. No doubt the post-Marian legions consisted mainly of *proletarii*, if only because most citizens belonged to this class. It is also often supposed that they were mostly volunteers. This is an illusion. In the decade that began in 90 the Italians under arms often numbered 250,000–300,000. From 78 to 49 the total oscillates between 60,000 and 150,000; the average is 90,000. In most of the next twenty years it exceeds 150,000, rising to 200,000. Volunteers could not fill the ranks, and in fact conscription is amply attested. Even commanders raising relatively small forces resorted to it, for instance Murena in 64, who required only to reinforce the legions in Gaul. Nor were men of property exempt. Pompey assumed in 49 that cohorts levied in Picenum had 'left their possessions behind them', and we hear in 41 of the fathers, sons or kin of soldiers who were being dispossessed of farms to make way for veterans (Dio XLVIII, 9).

The belief that volunteering had now become more common than the evidence warrants rests on the supposition that the soldier had a good chance of enrichment, not from his meagre pay, but from plunder, the donatives of generals and land allotments on discharge. Perhaps more men joined the army freely for such motives than in the past. But in some regions there was little plunder to be had, and generals were often incompetent; instead of enriching their armies, they destroyed them. There was no system for granting gratuities in cash or land to veterans. Men who had served under Sulla in the civil war of 83–81, under Pompey in 67–62 and under the victors in the civil wars of 49–30 received lavish gifts of money and allotments of land; this was a privilege they owed to the political dominance of their generals. The defeated had no such rewards, nor could the legionaries who served for years in provincial garrisons expect them; at best they might share in the booty obtained from the pacification of poor and barbarous tribes.

Conscription was detested at all times, especially in civil wars, when it was employed on the largest scale.

15

Cicero wrote of Caesar's levies in 49: 'even when conscription is imposed by good men, in a just war and with moderation, it is a hardship in itself, and what do you think must now be the case?' (*To Atticus* IX, 19, 1). It was at last abandoned in Italy by the emperor Tiberius; henceforth the government relied normally on provincial levies. By this time legionaries were better paid and entitled to fixed gratuities on discharge. Yet Italians gradually disappeared from the legions, a fair commentary on the supposed popularity of military service in the late Republic.

Writing of conditions that prevailed on the eve of Tiberius Gracchus' agrarian reform, Sallust says that 'a few men controlled everything in peace and war; they disposed of the treasury, the provinces, the magistracies, honours and triumphs; the people was oppressed by military service and by want; the booty of war fell into the hands of the generals and a few others. Meantime the parents or little children of the soldiers were driven out of their homes by powerful neighbours' (*Jugurthine War* 41). Appian (*Civil Wars* I, 7) says that the peasantry had been ruined by taxes and campaigns, and Gracchus lamented that men who had fought for Italy had become homeless vagrants with their wives and children (Plutarch, *Tiberius Gracchus* 9). Appian's allusion to the effect of taxation can refer only to the early second century, for from 168 the levy of a direct property tax on citizens was discontinued; public expenditure was now almost wholly met out of provincial revenues. The annalists who described social misery in early Rome constantly attributed it to the combined burden of taxation and conscription. They cannot have had any documentary evidence (Chapter 3), and though they may have found their authority in oral tradition, the details they give can only be the product of imagination inspired by later experience, and are relevant to conditions in the last two centuries of the Republic, when they were writing. Thus Livy, who drew on their accounts, tells that about 400, when the soldiers were kept under arms throughout the year for the war with Veii (just across the Tiber), they returned to find all their lands uncultivated for lack of the owners' care. That must indeed have been

16

the plight in the second century of many who spent six weary years in Spain. We are told that the consul, Marcus Atilius Regulus, asked to be relieved of his command in Africa in 256, because in his absence the bailiff of his little farm had died, the hired labourer had run off with the stock, and his wife and children were in danger of starving. Regulus, a noble, was surely a large landowner, and the story is fiction, yet fiction verified in the misfortunes of many common legionaries. Livy also has a story (II, 23) of an old soldier reduced to virtual servitude by debt because his lands had been ravaged, his farmhouse burned down, his cattle carried off while he was in the army; such must have been the fate of many Italian soldiers in the Hannibalic war and still more in the fighting which desolated parts of the peninsula in civil wars.

The progressive impoverishment of the peasantry was surely aggravated by wars and conscription. In conquering what they were pleased to call the world the Romans ruined a great part of the Italian people; naturally allies suffered as well as citizens. Meanwhile, as Sallust remarked, the upper classes grew richer. Immense profits were made by senators from booty, expense allowances and illicit exactions from Rome's subjects and by rich men outside the Senate, the Equites (pp. 69 ff.), from contracts for public works, army supplies and the collection of provincial taxes. In 160 Lucius Aemilius Paullus, who had conquered Macedon, died worth only 370,000 *denarii*; a man of scrupulous integrity, Polybius reckoned him poor for a senator (XXXI, 28; cf. XVIII, 35), yet his capital was 900 times that which was soon to be required of a legionary. In the next century Marcus Crassus' lands alone were valued at 50,000,000 *denarii*; he used to say that no one could be counted rich unless he could maintain an army from his income. Pompey and Caesar became richer still. Rome's expansion deepened the economic cleft between the classes.

The new wealth was partly squandered in luxury consumption, partly invested in Italian lands acquired from the poor by purchase, mortgages or sheer violence, and in slaves. As early as the first war with Carthage we hear that

20,000 prisoners were enslaved in Africa in 256 and 25,000 in one Sicilian city in 261. Aemilius Paullus is said to have sold 150,000 Epirotes in 167, and Caesar to have made 1,000,000 slaves in Gaul. These figures, particularly the last, cannot be relied on, but they illustrate the scale of enslavements which contemporaries found credible. War was not the sole source of slaves; for almost a century from about 167 piracy flourished in the east Mediterranean; the Romans long took no effective action against it, perhaps because their slave-owners were indirectly the beneficiaries; the free port of Delos, it is said, could handle 10,000 a day, and the pirates must have been the main suppliers. In 102 the king of Bithynia alleged that most of his subjects had been carried off into slavery by Roman tax-collectors. There was also traffic in slaves with peoples beyond the empire, and in many parts of the east free men would sell themselves or their children into slavery, when starvation was the only alternative. The practice, though forbidden to citizens by Roman law, may well not have been unknown in Italy itself. Exposure of infants was permitted, and the poor were probably often obliged to resort to it; most foundlings who survived were probably brought up as slaves. Because the rich had greater resources in Italy than elsewhere, thanks to the profits of empire, Italy was the principal importing country. Slaves laboured in the fields and in the workshops, as well as in domestic employment; they even predominated as secretaries, accountants and doctors. We do not know their numbers, but it may be *guessed* without implausibility that in 28 there were about 3,000,000 as against 4,000,000 free persons.[1] Probably the number of free persons had not increased over the previous two hundred years; the population had grown only by the accretion of slaves, while the free inhabitants themselves included several hundred thousand freedmen and others of partly servile stock.

Even as early as Hannibal's invasion the number of slaves must have been considerable, for it would otherwise have been quite impossible for Rome to mobilize for the armies and fleets one in every two of the citizens of

[1] See p. 1. About 1,000,000 citizens probably lived outside Italy.

18

military age; the necessary food and other supplies could not have been provided year by year but for slave labour. Only the abundance of such labour made it possible for the state to continue calling up so many free men in ensuing generations. Most labour was inevitably employed on the land, and on many great estates it consisted entirely of slave gangs. But the abundance of slaves also denied free men the chance of earning a decent living in peace. The small proprietor, ruined by service abroad, had difficulty in finding a job when he returned. With no regular employment, the poor could not afford to raise families. The free population failed to increase because the slave population multiplied. Astonished by what he read in the annals of the number of soldiers Rome had levied in fourth-century Latium, Livy concluded that there had once been an innumerable multitude of free men in places which in his day barely provided a tiny breeding ground for soldiers and were only redeemed from sheer emptiness by the slaves of the Romans (VI, 12).

The Background, The Roman Economy

IN considering the economy of any ancient people, we must rid ourselves of preconceptions natural in an age of extensive international trade and large-scale industry, fostered by cumulative capital investments and by an ever-faster flow of technical inventions. The basis of economic activity in antiquity was agrarian, and every district normally aimed at self-sufficiency. Trade was circumscribed outside a narrow radius to the exchange of luxury or semi-luxury goods or to such essential commodities as iron or salt, which were not found within that radius. Efforts also had to be made to import food in times of scarcity and exceptionally fertile regions, like Campania, generally had a surplus to sell. The most important local event of each year was usually the harvest, a fact still reflected in our harvest festivals; it might be ruined by drought, rains, floods or enemy ravaging; famine was an ever-present danger. Few peoples or cities could depend on regularly importing food; it was too precarious and costly. In the late Republic the city of Rome became one of the exceptions; it could bear the expense out of the profits of empire, but organization of supplies was difficult, and hunger was never far away. Industry hardly ever had extensive markets and did not need large factories even in great centres of population like Rome; when its products were made by hand with the aid of simple tools, there was no advantage in concentrating more workers in the same place than could easily be supervised by one man. Hence most production was carried on in small workshops by craftsmen who often sold their goods directly to the consumers.

Neither industry nor trade was socially esteemed at Rome. No person of repute is attested as having made his wealth by manufacturing, though of course landowners would exploit the resources of their estates; if suitable clay was to be found on them, they would establish kilns to make bricks or tiles, or fulling-mills; as early as 226 a consul (Gaius Apustius) was nicknamed the 'fuller', but it is significant that it was a gibe against Cicero that his father had profited from a fulling-mill on his property. Cicero also despised retail trading, on the moral pretext that it involved telling lies. Merchandise on a large scale was another matter in his eyes. Old Cato in the second century thought that trade might be more profitable than agriculture, but advised against it on the ground that it was so hazardous; one may think of Antonio in *The Merchant of Venice* and his lost argosies. Land was in Cato's view the safest investment, and Cicero recommended the successful merchant to buy an estate out of his profits; in Petronius' novel the freedman, Trimalchio, invested the huge gains of his maritime ventures in lands that stretched across Italy from sea to sea. 'Merchant' is never an honorific term in Latin. The explanation lay not merely in the conservative outlook of a society dominated by aristocratic landowners, but in economic considerations. In the last resort it was wealth that gave honour at Rome; even the most ancient nobility could not dispense with it, if their rank was to be preserved, and rich *parvenus* could over generations become their equals. But the opportunities of both acquiring *and preserving* wealth afforded by industry and trade were too limited and risky: there were no von Krupps or Henry Fords.

Surplus capital could indeed also be put out on loans. The practice of taking interest had once been disapproved or even forbidden. Cato remarked that the old way of thinking was made clear by laws which fined the thief double and the usurer fourfold. A century later moral scruples had vanished. The most eminent Romans practised usury. Marcus Brutus, that 'honourable man', lent to provincials at 48%, a rate partly dictated by the insecurity of the loan; among credit-worthy Romans interest might be as low as 4%. But most of these loans were probably given to tide men over brief periods in which they needed money for personal expenditure, perhaps also by patrons to set up their freedmen in shops or small factories. There were no such vast borrowing operations as those by which our trading and industrial companies find cash to expand their business. Nor was there any equivalent to these companies, owned by a multitude of shareholders with limited liability. Roman law only recognized partnerships in which each partner was liable for debts up to the hilt and which were dissolved at the wish or on the death of either partner. The one exception was made for the companies of public contractors, in which others besides the principals could take shares and which subsisted for the duration of the contract, normally five years; the state could not tolerate the sudden dissolution of companies performing essential public functions. There was also no national debt; the state paid its way out of current revenue and reserves of precious metal; consequently men could not accumulate capital in the public funds.

The return on land may well have been low and the possibilities of adding to landed wealth by improvement of an estate, as distinct from buying more acres, were limited by the unprogressive character of agriculture; after 200 indeed increased stockbreeding and planting of vines and olives in place of cereals probably raised profitability. The rich were tempted not to invest and accumulate but to spend, often even too profusely. Rank involved conspicuous consumption. The great houses were crowded with flunkeys, and their owners went out with a retinue. Under Nero the town house of an eminent senator contained 400 slaves; Tacitus remarks that in that age the luxury and ostentation of the Republic still survived. A political career almost necessitated prodigality, in provision of games, largesses of all kinds and even outright bribes. Meanness meant defeat at the polls. Extravagance extended beyond the grave. The heir was expected to give funeral games. Polybius (XXXI, 28) reports that in the second century they might cost 180,000 *denarii*, 1,500 times as much as a legionary's pay at the time. Under Augustus a rich freedman ordered 250,000 to be spent on his funeral (Pliny, *Natural History* XXXIII, 135). Men wished to leave a fair name behind them. Under the Principate we find benefactors in countless small towns

22

bequeathing money from which gifts of sweet wine and pastries were to be made in perpetuity on their birthdays.

This tendency to consume rather than to accumulate was linked with the lack of opportunities for productive investment, of which it was perhaps rather the consequence than the cause. There was little technological progress. The educated classes despised manual work and its operations as sordid. Perhaps this was because it was degraded by the prevalence of slave labour. Modern critics have also supposed that slave labour was unwilling and inefficient and that its apparent cheapness closed men's minds to the advantages of mechanical inventions. Yet there was no greater progress in provinces where few slaves were employed, nor in the Principate, when (it is commonly believed) slaves had become more costly, as the supply from war and piracy had diminished and it had become more often necessary to breed slaves and to bear the expense of maintaining children who might not live to working age. Moreover, skilled slaves had to be given the prospect of early enfranchisement as an incentive, and a motive for pursuing their masters' interests. Seneca says that they were responsible for many inventions, such as translucent windows, hot-water pipes in baths and shorthand (*Epistles* 90, 25).

Trade and, therefore, industry could not have developed on a larger scale unless there had first been great progress in transport. The Industrial Revolution in Britain was preceded by substantial improvements in the road and inland waterway systems and accelerated by the introduction of railways. Land transport was very backward in antiquity. We must not be misled by the Romans' skill in building paved roads, the first of which from Rome to Campania (Via Appia) goes back to the late fourth century. They were designed to facilitate the movement of armies; it is very doubtful how much they contributed to trade. It has been argued that they resembled not so much modern roads as stone walls; when they had been pitted by use, they could not be repaired but had to be rebuilt, a costly operation carried out at long intervals. It was indeed admittedly advantageous for a farm to lie near a great road, but these served only the main arteries of traffic, and in most districts it must have been necessary to carry goods over miles of rough track. However, the main obstacle to cheap transport by land lay not in the character of the roads, but in the methods used for haulage.[1] Until the early middle ages it was the universal practice to harness the horse with a soft collar round the throat instead of a hard collar round the chest; as a result he was throttled, the harder he pulled. The harness of oxen was relatively efficient; but they cannot pull as much as horses should be able to, and they move at only two miles an hour. In the late empire the maximum load permitted for carts in government service was no more than that of an unladen farm cart in the nineteenth century. Hence land transport was slow, inefficient and costly. Cato (*On Agriculture* 22) shows that it added about 2·5% per day to the prime cost of an oil-press weighing about 4,000 pounds to move it slowly by ox-team. In Diocletian's time (and it will have been no different in our period) the price of grain was increased by one-third or perhaps two-fifths, if it was transported fifty miles by cart. Over rough and mountainous country even carting was impossible. Varro tells how oil, wine and grain was brought down to the Apulian seaboard on donkey panniers. This is unlikely to have been cheaper.

If high costs were to be avoided, goods had to be transported by water. Rates quoted in the late empire show that 'it was cheaper to ship grain from one end of the Mediterranean to the other than to cart it 75 miles'.[2] Merchant ships were as large as many that used to cross the Atlantic; some may have been able to carry 200 tons. The emperor Claudius gave rewards to owners who would ply in the Roman grain trade, if their ships could carry 10,000 *modii*, about enough to feed 250 persons for a year. But seafaring was a risky business; there were no charts or compasses; the Mediterranean is a squally sea; and at times

---

[1] See Lynn White, *Mediaeval Technology and Social Change*, Oxford, Clarendon Press (1962), 57 ff.

[2] A. H. M. Jones, *The Later Roman Empire*, Oxford, Basil Blackwell (1964), II, 841 ff.

it was infested with pirates. In the winter navigation was normally suspended. Moreover, it is obvious that sea transport was of little benefit to people far from the coast, or rather from ports, in which the Italian littoral is deficient.

There remained transport by river or canal. But Italian like other Mediterranean rivers tend to be torrential after great rains or the melting of the snow and to dry up in the summer. In antiquity and the middle ages they may have been more navigable than to-day, perhaps because of greater humidity before so much of the mountain forest had been cut down. Certainly more use was made of them. South of the Po, the Tiber is by far the longest; yellow with the mud it brings down, and swollen by numerous tributaries, it winds for 250 miles from the Umbrian Apennines to its mouth at Ostia; the mean annual flow at Rome is over twice that to which it may be reduced in drought, and is exceeded fifteen times in floods; I have seen the wide and stony bed of the upper stream totally dried up, except for a few pools. The larger grain ships had to discharge their cargo into lighters in exposed water at the mouth, but sizeable vessels were hauled as far as Rome, and indeed small ships were towed far into the interior, up the tributaries as well as the Tiber itself. The strength of the current is such that they probably went up in ballast, but they brought cargo down, wheat, wine, timber, stone, sometimes from the upper course in Umbria. A few other rivers in peninsular Italy must have served trade in the same way though not to the same degree, and it was good advice to choose a farm near the coast or a navigable river. It is significant of the superiority of inland transport by water that Caesar began to build a canal parallel with the Appian Road, which even passengers preferred.

It was only in Cisalpine Gaul that the Po, Adige and their tributaries, supplemented by canals, offered a system of inland waterways comparable to those of England or northern Europe. Unfortunately, to say nothing of the calamitous floods to which they were subject and of silting at their outlet in the Adriatic, they gave access to the sea at a point far distant from the main centres of the Mediterranean world; it was not much further to Rome from Alexandria than from the mouth of the Po. In the first century AD Cisalpine Gaul was the most flourishing part of Italy; two centuries earlier, its abundant crops and cheap foodstuffs amazed Polybius (II, 15). Prices were low because the country had no foreign markets. To convey grain 50 miles or more across the Apennines to Genoa would have been prohibitive in cost, and seaborne grain from the mouth of the Po could not compete at Rome with that from nearer sources of supply, not only in Italy but in Sardinia, Sicily and Africa. Cisalpine Gaul perhaps always remained in antiquity a country to itself. It did, however, provide Rome with most of its pork, the only meat most people could ever afford. Pigs fed in the north could be driven to the capital; indeed in the first century AD even geese came that way from Flanders!

In the early Republic Rome obtained its grain from the surrounding country, or sometimes down the Tiber from Etruria and by sea from Campania or Sicily. From 200, as the population multiplied, local sources became more and more inadequate and the volume of seaborne imports increased; the farms nearby probably concentrated on wine, oil and garden products, which yielded higher profits. By AD 70 Rome depended mainly on the crops of Africa and Egypt in the proportion of 2 to 1; there is no evidence for regular imports from Egypt before its annexation in 30, and till then Sardinia and Sicily had been more important; in the Social war Campania was still the granary of the city. Rome could hardly live without imports, and the emperor Tiberius averred that Italy as a whole relied on them. His statement has been believed. Toynbee has graphically depicted how, as early as the second century, pasturage, vines and olives supplanted cereals almost everywhere; Dionysus expelled Ceres from the peninsula. This view is perfectly incredible. The city of Rome was fed at the expense of the subjects; imperial revenues were not available for other Italian towns. The costs of transportation made it inevitable that the inhabitants of the interior should grow their own food.

Cereal cultivation was ubiquitous; chaff, Columella observes, is often the only fodder for animals, but it may be found almost everywhere (VII, 1, 1). Some districts, like Campania and Apulia, were noted for their grain. The best of all came from Clusium (Chiusi) in Etruria, whence it probably still went down the Tiber to Rome. Roman writers on agriculture clearly indicate that the large owner could expect higher profits from wine, oil or pasturage, but that on large estates grain would be grown for consumption by the slave cultivators and herdsmen; since they must have aimed at producing enough even in a scarcity, when prices would rocket, in good or normal years they should have had a surplus to sell in neighbouring towns. Naturally too grain was grown by peasants producing less for the market than for family subsistence. If confirmation were needed of the continued importance of cereal cultivation, it can be found in the years when the pirates or Sextus Pompey interrupted seaborne supplies. There was famine, but the population did not perish *en masse*. The inhabitants of Rome itself mostly survived, and they must have been fed mainly, though doubtless inadequately, by Italian crops.

Each region was bound to seek self-sufficiency; even the great estates sought it. This was true not only of grain. In the Principate wine was produced in parts of Cisalpine Gaul where the soil and climate were unfavourable. The rich man could savour wine from Chios in crystalline goblets: most people drank *vin ordinaire* from local earthenware. Spinning and even weaving and clothes-making were domestic crafts. Great ladies boasted of their activity in weighing out the wool for their maids. The cloths made at Tarentum from the fine local fleeces and dyed red with the local mussels were for the rich. There was no equivalent of cheap Lancashire or Hong Kong cottons sold over the world. Commerce was confined to articles of prime necessity which could not be obtained at home, or to those which could still find a market after bearing heavy transport costs.

All this does not mean that trade was unimportant, even when it was not indispensable. No doubt among every

27

people the income from trade constituted a small part of what we should now call the national income, but for agrarian communities it was precisely the part which raised one state above the general level, which furnished a marginal superiority, and an excess of resources that might be used to assist in the aggrandisement of its power. The greatest wealth then came from the exercise of such power. Athens no doubt owed her rise to her mines, her olive oil, her shipping; for an ancient city she had a good deal of trade, and her exceptional economic prosperity enabled her to build a great fleet and to acquire an empire; but it was with the profits of empire that she built the Parthenon. The story of Rome is perhaps not wholly dissimilar; only the scale is vaster.

The low but defensible hills on which Rome grew up commanded the first point at which the Tiber could be bridged by methods known in antiquity and straddled the land route between Etruria and Campania, vital when the winter or hostile activity suspended communications by sea. The city was far enough from the sea to have early warning of maritime raiders, near enough to enjoy the benefit of seaborne supplies, while goods could also be shipped downstream from central Italy, and pans at the river mouth provided salt which went up-country to the Sabine lands. In the long run it was also important that Rome was strategically well-sited; by fairly easy passes armies could cross the mountains to the centre, east, north-east, and communications were smoother towards the south. But it was probably commerce that gave Rome a marginal advantage over neighbouring cities in her early history and enabled the primitive villagers of the eighth and seventh centuries, living in wattle and daub huts, to develop into the prosperous townsmen of the Etruscan monarchy, with houses of wood and brick, monumental temples, a well-engineered sewage system and imports of fine Attic vases. The Romans traced certain privileged corporations (*collegia*) of craftsmen to the early regal period—flautists, goldsmiths, carpenters, dyers, shoemakers, coppersmiths and potters; certainly they were very ancient, as they include no workers in iron, of whom there must have been many long before the Republic. But neither the existence of these corporations nor the archaeological evidence seems to prove that regal Rome was an industrial and exporting centre. Perhaps her prosperity rested chiefly, like that of early Corinth, on transit charges; and the recession that followed the fall of the Etruscan kings may then be explained by the disruption of trade, when land communications were cut between Etruria and her Campanion outpost and when the Latin plain was subjected to constant raids by mountain tribes. Economic decline may account for the bitter social strife described later. Rome reverted to being an almost purely agrarian community. The rich were the 'locupletes', those with abundance of land. But the land had always been the basis of the Roman economy.

There was no new wave of monumental building (of temples) until about 300. By then prosperity was the consequence of conquests and annexations. The first great step was the acquisition of the territory of Veii north of the Tiber; further conquests were retarded for a generation by the Gallic sack of Rome about 390 and then pursued with increasing vigour and success. In a certain sense Rome became a great commercial centre. This development was consequent on and proportionate to the growth of her power. Naturally the city had always had a market (every ninth day) in which the surrounding peasants sold their produce and bought what they needed from the urban craftsmen. In the second century Cato recommended buying at Rome tunics, togas, cloaks, patchwork cloth and wooden shoes (though some of these things were also made on his estates), as well as jars, bowls, ploughs, yokes, locks and keys and the best baskets, but many such articles could also be purchased in country towns; whether you went to Rome for them depended on the distance. Later we find districts or streets named after potters, silversmiths, grain merchants, sandal-makers, timber merchants, log-sellers, perfumers and scythemakers; men of one craft tended to congregate. The manufacture of arms must have been particularly important; legions were often mobilized at Rome, and sometimes drilled there for a year. Warships too were built and docked in the Tiber, and the great fleets of the wars with Carthage were equipped there. The magnates had town-houses and ever-increasing domestic staffs. There were so many more to feed, clothe and house. Hence, more and more dock labourers and porters and, as the pace of public and private constructions accelerated, more building workers. Requirements correspondingly rose for retailers and craftsmen of all kinds. The city grew upon itself. The concentration of the riches of the empire in the hands of a few Romans also meant that it was at Rome that loans were most easily to be secured; it became the leading banking centre. Rome was parasitic on the whole Mediterranean world: it was quite untypical of Italy, and most Romans did not live in it. Those who did mostly drew their income from Italian estates, or directly or indirectly from imperial profits; food subsidies for the poor, like the public and private building activity, were ultimately a charge on provincials.

In the meantime, as shown in the first chapter, Rome was enlarging her territory in Italy. Ancient writers extol Italy for her fertile soil and temperate climate, her rivers, lakes, forests, minerals, pastures and game. Under Augustus, the Greek historian Dionysius of Halicarnassus claimed that she had a sufficiency of every product men needed. Some years earlier, Varro had described the whole land as an orchard. These panegyrics are absurdly exaggerated. Italy was deficient in minerals, despite valuable iron deposits on Elba; by the second century her needs were being met especially from Spanish mines. Of the rivers enough has been said. Much more of the country was then under forest; the abundance of timber was valuable to the nation and must have been an important source of income to individual owners. Land was no doubt constantly being cleared, and the virgin soil yielded heavy crops; the disastrous erosion so visible today on Italian hillsides was often a delayed effect; for the time being more food could be produced to support a population that was growing, though only because of the mass importation of slaves. But in the late nineteenth century 45% of the surface was uncultivated, and the proportion was probably higher in antiquity. Much of the soil too was very poor; there were no artificial fertilizers; farmers had to rely mainly on compost, for manure was inadequate, as it was generally impossible to grow fodder for many animals as well as human food; the transhumance system (p. 33) meant that the droppings of half the year were wasted. Except in the most fertile areas, fields generally had to lie fallow every alternate year. In the late Republic men were complaining that the soil was exhausted by old age and in the next century Columella estimated that the average return on grain sown was only fourfold; of this about a quarter would have been required for seed. Data from mediaeval and early modern times suggest that his estimate need not have been too pessimistic, though by the late nineteenth century yields were often twice as great. The ancient encomia really show only that Italy was not so poor in natural resources as most other Mediterranean lands.

However, in their annexations the Romans were apt to take the best land for themselves or the Latins and leave the worst to the allies. By the third century there were stretches of Roman territory southwards to the border of Campania, including the rich Falernian land, where some of the noblest Italian wine was made. The incorporation of Capua about 338 brought in north Campania with the most fertile soil in Italy; it was of this country that Virgil sang,

> fulfilled with heavy corn and
> Campanian wine, possessed by olives and prosperous
>   herds. . . .
> Here is continual spring and a summer beyond her
>   season;
> Cattle bear twice yearly, apples a second crop[1]

Capua revolted to Hannibal; as a punishment her people were deprived of the ownership of their land, much of which they continued to till as tenants of the state; somehow (the facts are obscure) Roman magnates encroached on the public property and made handsome profits. A part of it also went to new Roman colonies, including

[1] C. Day Lewis' translation of *Georgis* II, 143 ff.

Puteoli (Pozzuoli); as return cargoes could be obtained here and not at Rome or Ostia, and as many vessels could not get up the Tiber, much produce for Rome was unloaded and probably transhipped in this natural port, which became one of the most thriving towns in Italy. The valley of the Volturnus too was Roman; here Venafrum produced the finest olive oil. Substantial tracts of the Etruscan coast which had also been annexed were less useful; much of this country was swampy and fever-ridden, and in 137 Tiberius Gracchus found it almost deserted except for slaves. Another great stretch of Roman territory extended across central Italy through the Sabine lands, where the Veline lake was drained soon after 290 to provide virgin soil for new settlements, to Picenum on the Adriatic. Between 218 and 173 Gauls and Ligurians had to surrender more territory to Roman and Latin colonists in Emilia (the modern name comes from a consul of 187) and Piedmont; the cities of Placentia (Piacenza), Cremona, Parma, Mutina (Modena) and Bononia (Bologna) were founded in this period, and were destined to enjoy exceptional prosperity.

No part of Roman territory was subjected to any prolonged devastations in the Hannibalic war, except for Campania which soon recovered. The war was fought mainly on allied territory in the south, where it caused enormous destruction and loss of life. Here most of the country consists of mountains, now often eroded but then thickly forested, or of hills and upland plateaux with a relatively poor soil; in 280 king Pyrrhus of Epirus had contrasted its poverty with the orchards of the Romans. Most of the southern peoples revolted to Hannibal, and Rome punished their disloyalty by sequestrating great tracts of their territory, often including the few rich valleys or plains. The newly annexed land was little needed for Roman settlement, and much was probably exploited for pasturage by the Roman magnates. The wretchedness of the Mezzogiorno in modern Italy has a parallel in its desolation under the Roman Republic.

The story is told that the elder Cato said that the best investments were, in order of preference, good pasture lands, middling pasture lands, poor pasture lands, arable. If every one had followed this supposed recommendation, its purpose would have been defeated; the market for wool, hides, cheese and meat would soon have been saturated, particularly as the standard of life for the slaves and free poor was low; Cato's slaves received a tunic and a blanket every other year, and they ate no meat. (No one ate butter, and milk was not much drunk.) Stockbreeding is more economical of labour than agriculture, but that was relatively unimportant when there was an abundance of cheap imported slaves. However, there is no doubt that stockbreeding now received a great impetus. Throughout the centuries it has rested in Italy on the transhumance system, which is only now dying out. Every summer when the snows melt, the herds trail upwards to graze on the verdant herbage of the woods or high plateaux of the Apennines; every autumn they return to the valleys or coastal plains; in antiquity they migrated from the central Apennines to Apulia or from the Lucanian mountains to the Calabrian coast. Winter pasturage was also found in Latium and Campania; our earliest clear record of the system is a model contract Cato gives for leasing it, and he farmed in those parts. Transhumance may have been practised by the Romans from very early times, but only the pacification of Italy and then the confiscation of large areas in the south can have promoted it on a large scale. For the first time rich Romans had at their disposal in the winter rich low-lying land which they could graze without regard to the interests of the erstwhile cultivators, who were not citizens with votes but conquered rebels. The land indeed belonged to the state, and the state imposed fees per head of cattle grazed on it, but the fees, fixed by members of the class which stood to gain, will not have been high.

Thus in some parts of Italy sheep drove out men. But elsewhere the arable area was probably extended by clearance of forests and drainage of marshes; more land came under vines and olives. The vine had been planted near Rome under the monarchy, the olive (as its name shows) was imported from Greece; we do not know when.

On the whole it was the well-to-do who gained, because only they could afford to wait for returns on the capital invested; the vine does not give a full yield for a few years, and the olive (which bears only in alternate seasons) not for a generation. Land was the safest and most socially acceptable way of investing the profits made in war and government; the rich had every motive to grab what they could from impoverished peasants. Thus smallholdings tended to be absorbed in large estates (*latifundia*), though they never totally disappeared. From a moral and social standpoint the elder Pliny held that *latifundia* had long ago ruined Italy (*Natural History* XVIII, 35). Economically, they may have added to her wealth. New ideas were introduced by Greek and Carthaginian treatises and perhaps by skilled slaves from the east and Africa. However, most owners were absentees, who left everything to bailiffs and slave-gangs and, ignorant of agricultural techniques, cared only for the income; they were seldom active improvers, unlike many great noble landlords of eighteenth- and nineteenth-century England.

How big were the *latifundia*? In 49 Lucius Domitius Ahenobarbus offered to perhaps 10,000 soldiers 40 *iugera* apiece from his own property (Caesar, *Civil Wars* I, 17); he may then have owned over 400,000, about 270,000 acres. A wealthy freedman, Isidorus, who died in AD 8, claimed to have had 3,600 pairs of oxen, enough to have ploughed 360,000 *iugera* (Pliny, *Natural History* XXXIII, 135). Cicero refers in 63 to a man of no great note who had acquired possession of a whole 'region' (*On the Agrarian Law* III, 8), and there are many later allusions to such vast estates. At first sight it is then surprising that the writers on agriculture, whose works were meant for the rich, describe standard farms of 100–240 *iugera* and that the farms excavated near Pompeii also seem to be of this relatively small size. However, many rich men had property in different regions; Cicero, for instance, possessed several small farms in the territory of his native Arpinum and estates in seven or eight other places. By buying up contiguous land, an owner could economize in expenditure on his villas or farmhouses and their outbuildings, but

34

he might think it more prudent, as Pompey did, to distribute the risks of climatic conditions. A unit of 100–200
iugera could conveniently be managed by a bailiff, super-
vising a dozen slaves, and its small size is no proof that the
owner was not a man of great landed wealth. Stockbreeding required the enjoyment of the most extensive
areas. Isidorus claimed to have owned 257,000 animals
other than oxen, i.e. sheep, goats and pigs. Some of these
were doubtless fed on public or leased land, as well as on
his own property. In the second century the law (which
was not observed) prescribed that a man might not graze
more than 100 oxen or horses nor more than 500 sheep,
goats and pigs on *public* land. Modern statistics suggest
that for so many oxen or sheep about 1,800 *iugera* were
required. Isidorus might well have needed 300,000, or
many more of poor pasturage. Flocks might be no more
than 100 strong; again owners preferred units which one
shepherd could manage; they could have many such
flocks.

Ordinary citizens, we are told, had once had no more
than seven or even two *iugera*, and some allotments in
second-century colonies comprised only five to ten. Except
on unusually fertile soil, such small farms could not have
assured the subsistence of a family. On the evidence we
have for soldiers' and slaves' rations a family of four might
have consumed about 144 *modii* or pecks of wheat a year,
for which vegetables could be substituted in part. Columella says that between five and ten pecks were sown *per
iugerum* on medium land and that the average return was
under fourfold. Probably small farms were more inten-
sively cultivated than the great estates of which he knew
most, and his estimate may be too pessimistic. Let us
assume then that 10 *modii* were sown, and that 50 were
reaped, of which 10 had to be kept back for seed. However, if the yield were not to fall disastrously, most land
had to be fallowed every other year. Thus the net average
yield *per iugerum* was not 40, but 20 *modii*, and a farm of
7 *iugera* barely produced enough grain for consumption by
the family, with no fodder for animals, no fruits, no margin
for sales out of which other necessities could be obtained.

35

It seems probable then that such small owners must have eked out a living by working at daily rates on great estates, by leasing additional parcels of land and by exercising rights to pasture pigs and gather wood on domain land, or perhaps even to enclose and cultivate it. Always precarious, their position became untenable if they were denied such opportunities, or if they were for long taken from the plough to serve in the army, leaving the tillage to wives and children. Even in bumper years, they could seldom follow Cato's recommendation and hold back the sale of surplus produce until prices had somewhat risen; they had no reserve and could not build one up. And what would happen in bad years may be imagined with the help of a petition of French peasants in 1789: 'A peasant in hard times is dazzled with the offer of ready cash; difficulties are brought upon him by a cruel generosity in lending to him until he cannot repay what he has borrowed. Then his land is seized and sold at a low price to the advantage of the creditor.'[1] The rich might not even await such opportunities; expropriation by sheer violence became common. Their political control also enabled them to deny to the poor a fair share in the public domain.

From the Hannibalic war the great landowners relied increasingly on slaves both to cultivate their fields and to tend their herds. Cato and later writers on agriculture simply assume that the permanent labour force on large estates normally consists of slaves; at most they recommend leasing farms to free tenants, if they are too distant for the owners to exercise constant supervision, or if the land is unhealthy; a high mortality raised unduly the depreciation costs of slaves. There are indeed a few indications that free tenants were more common in the late Republic than has generally been assumed, but slave labour undoubtedly predominated, subject to one qualification: it was uneconomic for an owner to support throughout the year as many labourers as he needed for the short seasons of most intensive effort. Hence free

[1] Quoted from A. Cobban, *The Social Interpretation of the French Revolution*, Cambridge University Press (1968), 155.

labourers were hired by the day for the harvest, vintage and picking and crushing of olives. This seasonal employment was available to smallholders near a large estate, but it was also one of the few sources of income for the landless.

For that class, always large and growing after 200, there was also casual work in the towns. But here too employers seem to have preferred slaves for work that went on steadily throughout the year. Some slaves probably brought special skills with them from the east; others were specially trained; in the crafts unskilled workers from the country could not compete, and even the native free artisans seem to have been displaced. Gravestones, our main evidence, suggest that at Rome perhaps no more than 10% of the artisans were of free birth. The proportion is not much higher in small towns; we find none at all among those who made the fine pottery of Arezzo (Arretium), which captured the markets of the empire under Augustus. The bulk of evidence is later than our period, but less copious statistics from Republican and Augustan inscriptions alone yield similar results. It cost money to put up a tombstone, and the majority of the artisans who did so were freedmen; they had presumably made good and earned manumission in the same crafts they had practised as slaves. That gave them something to be proud of, and they may have been keener to commemorate themselves than the poor of free birth, or the latter may have had less means to do so. However, the literary evidence too strongly suggests that freedmen and slaves preponderated numerically at Rome, and there the free-born poor perhaps numbered in the 70s only a fifth of the free population (p. 120). Most of them probably subsisted on seasonal work, for instance in the docks; since shipping almost ceased in the winter, the work bunched in a few months of the year, and no rational person would have maintained permanent gangs of slave dockers. The scale of building activity also fluctuated widely; we know that contractors had slave workers, but they surely supplemented them in booms with free labourers; in 44 we find free men at work on one of Cicero's villas near Rome. Popular leaders were often responsible for new public building programmes, surely in order to create opportunities for employment.

In general slave competition must have caused severe unemployment or chronic under-employment among the free poor. What were they to do? It has been supposed that many migrated. We hear a good deal of Italians in the east in the last two centuries of the Republic, and probably they were still more numerous in western provinces. In Asia alone Mithridates, king of Pontus, is said to have massacred 80,000; the figure might well be divided by ten. These Italians overseas were mainly tax-farmers, bankers, traders, even landowners; many were allies, not citizens, before 90; most were probably their staff, freedmen or slaves. The number of free men in business overseas was doubtless significant, economically and socially, in relation to the communities where they lived, but absolutely it cannot have been great. No doubt soldiers sometimes settled in areas where they were stationed, for instance in Spain, but in the civil wars it was hard to conscribe many Italian recruits overseas, and I cannot believe that any substantial emigration by the poor was practicable except with governmental direction and support, such as Caesar was the first to afford on any large scale. How was the individual peasant to find land in an unfamiliar country, to acquire and stock it when he had no resources, or to maintain himself there amidst resentful foreign neighbours? These difficulties could hardly ever be overcome except when the state marked out and provided the land, equipped the farms and settled the emigrants in colonies walled against attack, in which hundreds or thousands could help to defend each other. It may be said that it was not inevitable that the emigrants should earn their living primarily on the land. Perhaps not; but we have no ground for thinking that small men left Italy to become shop-keepers, traders or craftsmen overseas. And everywhere agriculture was the basis of the economy.

Only agriculture was not the main reason for the immensity of Roman wealth. Still less were trade and industry. The most lucrative business of the Romans was war and government. At first war had to be paid for: later it more than paid for itself

Until 167 the state collected yearly from the *assidui* (p. 11) a capital levy of 0·1%; in great wars higher rates were imposed, but as forced loans, to be repaid as soon as possible from the profits of victory. Thus, the extra sums levied in the Hannibalic war were all repaid out of booty and indemnities from the conquered fourteen years after its close. Even this *tributum* (we are told) was one cause of impoverishment. The tax was 'regressive', charged to all at the same rate, and when the rate was high, it was burdensome to those who were relatively poor; repayment might be deferred too long to save them from ruin. In 167 *tributum* was suspended, and henceforth the only taxes which fell on citizens were low customs duties (abolished temporarily in 60), and taxes on sales by auction and on the value of slaves manumitted. The treasury was mainly fed by provincial revenues. By 74 they amounted to 50 million *denarii* a year and by 62, after Pompey's annexations in the east, to 135 millions.

Where did the money go? These sums are equivalent respectively to annual wages for over 400,000 and over 1,100,000 private soldiers. Except in civil wars the actual wage bill cannot have reached 12 million *denarii*. In addition there was the cost of military supplies, partly deducted from soldiers' wages. Expenditure on public works fluctuated; the most costly building we know of, and perhaps the most costly before Caesar, was the Marcian aqueduct, completed over five years (144–140) for 45 millions. There were also games, and after 123 subsidies (withdrawn or greatly reduced at times) for corn-doles at Rome. Once grain was distributed quite free (in 58), and to an in-increased number of recipients (from 62), Cicero reckoned that they took a fifth of the revenue, 27 millions a year, but before 62 the cost must have been quite low. We cannot draw up a budget, but it looks as if there should have been even before 62 a large surplus. Yet we often hear that the treasury was short of funds.

There can be only one explanation, the lavish expense allowances for the unpaid governors and their staffs. In one year as governor of Cilicia Cicero saved 550,000 *denarii*.

He had broken no law; he boasted with justice of his integrity. Others added to their gains by peculation from the public purse and extortion from the subjects. Booty was another source of enrichment. The ordinary soldiers usually participated, though there were complaints as early as 195 that generals kept it all for themselves and their friends; certainly the commander and his staff always had the lion's share. Pompey treated his men with exceptional liberality in the east, but on one distribution there the military tribunes, who came from the higher classes, received 120 times as much as the privates. Pompey himself became the richest man at Rome. After his death his estates were valued at 50 millions. Tax-farmers too had a handsome legal rake-off before remitting revenue to the treasury, not to speak of what they made by illicit exactions.

The profits of empire enabled the upper classes to import hundreds of thousands of slaves, whole cargoes of Greek art, luxuries of every kind, and to buy up lands, stock them with cattle or turn them into the orchards Varro admired. 'If there is no justice,' wrote St. Augustine (*City of God* IV, 4), 'what are kingdoms but robbery on a large scale?' The Roman ruling class practised it on the largest scale yet known; they robbed their subjects abroad, so that they could better rob their fellow-countrymen.

By modern standards the ancient world was always poor and 'under-developed'. If any progress was to be made, it was inevitable that the majority should hew and carry in order that a very few might have the means and leisure to cultivate the arts and sciences. Even in democratic Athens property was unequally distributed; slave labour supported the wants of poets and philosophers and enabled quite humble citizens to devote some of their energy to war and government. Plato had said that in his day, the fourth century, every city was divided into the city of the rich and the city of the poor, just as Disraeli said that in nineteenth-century England there were 'two nations'. What distinguished Rome was neither economic inequality nor exploitation but the enormity in the scale of both. Whether or not this be deemed a fit matter for moral condemnation, the facts are of the highest historical importance, for revolution was to spring from the misery and resentment of the masses.

The earliest social conflicts in Rome, however, occurred, and the social and political order of the imperial Republic took shape, in a small, struggling, agrarian community, in which even the rich were by later criteria only middling proprietors (though perhaps no noble Cincinnatus was ever called, dusty from the plough, to save the state), and it is to this formative era that we must first devote attention.

3

Plebeians versus Patricians, 509–287

THE early history of Rome is obscure; modern accounts freely contradict each other, and all are in some degree conjectural. Until the third century Rome attracted little attention from the contemporary Greek world, and the first Roman chronicle of the city was written by a patrician, Fabius Pictor, as late as 200. Only a few fragments survive of his work and of that of later Republican annalists. Our knowledge of early Rome comes mainly from the histories of Livy and Dionysius of Halicarnassus written under Augustus; they drew principally on annals composed after the Gracchi or Sulla. We have to ask what evidence lay before Fabius and his successors.

By the time the monarchy fell the Romans were certainly literate; laws and treaties were written down. However, they themselves believed that most early documents perished in the Gallic sack of Rome (*c.* 390), and though some allegedly earlier texts have been preserved by ancient authors, their dating or authenticity is in doubt, apart from the numerous fragments of the Twelve Tables, the law code of *c.* 450, which Roman boys used to learn by heart; they are our most precious evidence for the fifth century. It was the Roman custom to date legal or other transactions by the names of the consuls; for instance, an event we put in 63 was said to have occurred in the consulship of Marcus Tullius Cicero and Gaius Antonius. A list of the principal magistrates was, therefore, necessary for practical life, and this list, the *Fasti*, purports to go back to 509; it was the chronological basis of the Roman annals, which are so called because they recorded transactions year by year. Probably it is sound in the main almost from the beginning. The priestly college of pontiffs also used to issue daily notices of certain events on whitened tablets; their contents were collected and published late in the second century. This published version pretended to go

42

back to the foundation of Rome, and obviously contained much legend added later to genuine records, which perhaps began not before 300. Moreover, Cato said that the tablets were full of what he regarded as trivialities, notices of dearths or eclipses, and perhaps they were of little use to those like Fabius who aimed at writing political history.

It seems beyond question that the early annalists had to rely chiefly on tradition, especially that preserved in the great houses, by word of mouth through successive generations. When a Roman noble died, men wearing masks of his ancestors and their official dress paraded at the funeral, and a kinsman or friend pronounced an oration in which he commemorated the achievements of these ancestors as well as those of the deceased. But oral tradition was often distorted by patriotic or family pride, and even by the malice of one house to another. And it was also enriched by the Roman gift for inventing stories in vivid details, a gift they did not express like the Greeks in tales of gods and heroes, but applied to real or fictitious persons in a particular historical context; the stories often inculcated moral and political lessons. Fabius' annals were already full of mere legends about the regal period. His account of the early Republic was meagre; his successors enormously enlarged it, at a time when even less could be remembered. Imagination was fertilized by contemporary experience; anachronisms can be detected; the political propaganda of the Gracchan or Sullan ages was shifted into a remote past.

It may then seem a desperate enterprise to recover the truth about the fifth and fourth centuries. However, the tradition can be controlled by scraps of other evidence of varying kinds; pieces of ancient ritual, the meaning of technical terms, the character of Rome's historic institutions which in itself reveals something of their past, analogies with other peoples. Much that we are told must be rejected as incoherent, much doubted on the ground that no memory of it would probably have been preserved; the arguments and slogans of party leaders, and many graphic particulars of political and social conflicts can often be exploited only in reconstructing later times. Some scholars pin their faith on selected details and use them to discredit the tradition in its broadest features; they then arbitrarily accept what they please, and present a story as fictitious as Livy's, though less entertaining. By contrast, my own sketch, sceptical of details, will be deliberately conservative of the tradition's outlines which were probably transmitted correctly.

We are told that Rome was at first ruled by an elective king; on his death his power passed to an 'interim-king' (*interrex*), until a permanent successor was appointed. Analogies support the tradition, and in the Republic there were still 'interim-kings', who held the annual elections, if the outgoing pair of consuls had failed to do so. A royal election required the assent both of the people in arms, given by acclamation, and of the council of elders, to give the 'Senate' its original sense; in the Republic men of thirty or even twenty-five were admitted. The Senate seems once to have consisted of heads of households and was, therefore, also called 'patres'; in historic times, however, father and son could sit together. The senators constituted the king's council, but like the magistrates in the Republic he was not formally bound by their advice. He had *auspicium*, the right to ascertain the will of the gods by prescribed rituals, and it was perhaps as the intermediary with heaven that he was supreme on earth. He commanded in war and had jurisdiction over life and death; these military and judicial prerogatives were summed up by the Romans in the term *imperium*; the general was an *imperator*, the word from which our 'emperor' derives, and which the Greeks translated as *autocrator*, 'possessed of absolute power'. By its nature *imperium* was despotic, and the Romans often contrasted it with *libertas*, freedom. According to tradition the last king, Tarquin the Proud, exercised power tyrannically and was overthrown by the nobility. In historic Rome the very word *regnum* (kingship) had an evil sound, and it was the most bitter of reproaches to say that a man aimed at securing it. It is immensely plausible that tradition is correct, though some have impugned it, and that the mon-

44

archy was destroyed by a revolution and did not fade away gradually.

The Romans substituted for the king two magistrates, later named consuls, who held office only for a year and were not immediately re-eligible. They inherited the royal power, and Cicero could still say that their highest law was the public safety; in principle they had discretion to do what they thought best. But the mere fact that they were annual magistrates had enormous consequences. They could be brought to account when they laid down office, and as they held it for so short a time, they were much more likely to defer to the will of the Senate. Membership of the Senate was for life; they themselves were senators, and it was in their own interest in the long run to aggrandize the authority of a body in which they had a permanent voice rather than that of a magistracy they were so soon to lose. Moreover, by a peculiar convention, if the consuls disagreed, the negative view prevailed, and it would go hard for the Senate, only if both of them conspired to ignore its wishes. Thus collegiality in itself weakened the force of *imperium* and contributed, as the Romans saw, to *libertas*. In emergencies, until the end of the third century, the Romans would still appoint a single man as dictator to exercise overriding power, but he held office for only six months, and the dislike of autocracy was so strong that none ever dared exceed that limit.

In course of time the multiplication of business made it necessary to elect other annual magistrates, quaestors to assist in financial administration, aediles to supervise the buildings, streets and markets of the city, praetors to do justice at Rome and later to govern overseas provinces; men ascended this ladder of promotion stage by stage. Praetors and consuls often had to be given extension of commands over armies and in provinces for one or several years after the expiry of their office; they were propraetors or proconsuls. Men who had already held the consulship might reach the apogee of their official careers as censors; they were charged every five years with registering the citizens at a census, making up the roll of the senate,

45

letting out public contracts and scrutinizing the morals of the citizens. But the consuls always remained heads of the state.

They were not, however, formally sovereign and they did not hold the reality of power.

Sovereignty in a certain sense belonged to the people. The people alone elected magistrates, declared war, made treaties and passed laws. Yet the people could meet only on the summons of one of the higher magistrates, vote only on the proposals he chose to submit, select candidates from a list he set before it, and say only 'Yea' or 'Nay' to a law he proposed; it might contain hundreds of clauses, but no amendment was possible. There would be a preliminary debate, but no one could speak except on the invitation of the summoning magistrate, though other magistrates might also convene meetings for discussion and ask the views of different persons. All this remained true throughout the Republic.

The assemblies of the people were also far from democratic. A majority was obtained not by counting heads but by counting units. There was more than one kind of assembly; here we shall speak only of the centuriate, in which the voting units were 'centuries', originally battalions of fighting men. The centuries were divided by property classes, and 98 out of 193 at first consisted of citizens who belonged to the highest class or (what came to the same thing) served in the cavalry. If they were in unanimous agreement, the remaining centuries were not even called. Citizens who had virtually no property, the *proletarii*, formed only a single century, which voted last, if at all.

The centuries seldom met; legislation was infrequent and later fell normally to a different assembly; wars were commonly not declared but were represented, more or less truly, as defensive. The regular and indispensable task of the centuries was that of electing the magistrates. This was indeed of the highest importance; elections not only decided who were to be the executive agents of the state; they gave the successful candidates lasting prestige in the counsels of the Senate. In Rome influence (*auctoritas*) had

46

hardly less weight than official power; it belonged to the Senate as such, and within the Senate to its leading men (*principes*), who owed their eminence partly to their birth or talents, partly to the honours the people had conferred on them.

The Senate and the *principes* had the reality of power. Nominally advisory, the Senate did not instruct magistrates, but suggested a course they might take, 'if they saw fit'. In practice its suggestions could not be disregarded; meeting frequently, discussing everything, the senators with their social prestige and accumulated experience assumed direction of the state; they were, as the envoy of Pyrrhus of Epirus put it, 'an assembly of kings', and Cicero laid it down as an accepted rule of the constitution that the magistrates were to be the servants of the Senate (*For Sestius* 137).

In the early Republic the magistrates at least were exclusively patricians, who also dominated the Senate. We do not know the origin of the patricians nor of their monopoly of power. They were a closed order throughout the Republic; no one was a patrician whose male ancestors had not all been patricians, and in early times they tried to prohibit intermarriage with the other citizens, the plebeians or men of the masses (*plebs*). The distinction was one of birth, not wealth; the conflict of the orders is unintelligible unless there were rich plebeians, but no doubt property was originally concentrated more in the hands of the patricians. For this reason, and also because they controlled the government, the patricians were held up to opprobrium for the miseries of the poor; the rich plebeians, who desired to gain a share in political power, from time to time made themselves the champions of their oppressed brethren. It was not until 366 that the consulship was opened to them. Yet the patricians were very few; after 366 only twenty-one clans are attested, of which some were tiny, and not more than another score before that date. A diminution in their numbers no doubt helps to explain why they ultimately had to give in, but it is puzzling that they held out for so long. One reason may be sought in the relations of dependence and deference,

which never ceased to operate in Roman society throughout the Republic.

The relations which should obtain between the classes in
the eyes of Roman aristocrats were realized, according to
Velleius (II, 126), under the emperor Tiberius: 'the
humble look up to the powerful without fear, while the
powerful do not despise the humble.' This ideal was
served by the ties between patron and client. Except
between the patron and his former slave, who remained
under legal obligations to his old master, these ties in
later Rome were simply moral. A client 'commended himself' (a term still used in mediaeval vassalage) to the 'faith'
of his patron. Good faith, of which the Romans boasted,
was the basis of many legally enforceable transactions, but
its scope was not limited to acts which could give rise to
suits in the courts. It also demanded that good services
should be requited. The Roman advocate, who was
actually called a patron, was not permitted fees, but could
expect grateful clients to recompense him by other services and even by legacies; Cicero received 5,000,000
denarii from bequests in thirty years. Morally, patrons
and clients were obliged to assist each other in every
legally permissible way. At all times, patrons would give
their clients legal advice and appear in the courts on
their behalf, or settle their disputes by arbitration.
Patrons and clients could not bring charges or even bear
witness against each other. Clients were expected to
escort their patron in public, adding to his prestige in
proportion to their numbers, and to vote for him; it is
said that in old days they would help to provide dowries,
pay fines and ransoms, and meet election costs. In civil
war Pompey raised an army mainly from his clients
(83), and in the riots of the 50s he called them up from
Picenum and Cisalpine Gaul to defend his person and do
battle on the streets with hostile gangs. The relation was
hereditary. The most powerful families counted among
their clients cities, provinces and foreign princes, not to
speak of rich Romans outside the magisterial class, whom
it was indeed tactful to dignify with the name of friends.
A magnate could mobilize in his support not only his own

dependents but those of others with whom he was allied at the time. Many communities and individuals, however, had more than one patron; if the patrons fell out, they had to choose between them, and they might do so on considerations of public interest (which, of course, was always supposed to prevail over any private ties) or of their own safety and advantage.

We are told that originally all plebeians were clients of the patricians, and though by the early Republic many plebeians were evidently free of clientage (conceivably those who were descended from clients of the banished kings or of patrician families that had become extinct) the great houses had numerous retainers; the story went that the Fabii carried on the city's war with Veii for seven years, assisted only by their clients. The annalists believed that the patricians were often backed by their clients against the rest of the plebs. Though this belief may have been suggested by the experience of later times rather than by genuine tradition, it was surely correct. The bonds between patron and client were tighter in early Rome than they became later; under the Twelve Tables a patron who defrauded his client was accursed and could be killed with impunity, a rule later obsolete. A man was supposed to put his clients before his own kin by marriage. The system of dependence was politically important in the first century, and must have been much stronger in the fifth.

It could only have originated in a society in which economic and political power was very unevenly distributed. Once it existed, it tended to perpetuate itself. Ties accepted under iron necessity acquired moral force. In each generation some escaped from clientage by rising economically and socially, but others fell into it, for power was still concentrated in a few hands, and the humble still needed protection. In particular, justice was always administered by the upper class; the courts might be susceptible to influence, or even bribes; the law's delays worked against the poor; and a plaintiff had personally to bring a defendant into court and, if he won, to execute judgement without aid at any point from the coercive power of the state. It is no wonder that most men had to lean on patrons, without whose help they might have small prospect of redress against a wrongdoer, at once more powerful and devoid of scruple.[1]

We may then well imagine that the patricians retained their monopoly so long because of the great number of their clients. But perhaps there was another reason. In the late Republic candidates for office seldom, if ever, stood on programmes; they solicited votes for their personal merits, or when these were trifling or unknown (as might often be the case), on the services their ancestors had rendered to the state. Cicero says that 'all of us good men always favour the nobility' (*For Sestius* 21), yet he was an upstart himself. Few *parvenus* were known to the electorate for their talents; none perhaps commended themselves by advocating popular policies in advance; all belonged to the wealthy class, since it was costly to embark on a political career; it was natural for the voters to prefer, as between two rich candidates, one who could point to the fame of his ancestors. In the early Republic only the patricians were nobles. Even when admitted to office by law, rich plebeians could hardly compete, unless they made themselves popular champions, which they were seldom disposed to do, as their economic interests were in general those of the patricians. In 366 they insisted that it be prescribed that one consul should always be a plebeian, and even so in many subsequent years the voters defied the law and chose two patricians.

But for its oppressive character patrician rule might have lasted longer. We must believe in the tradition that there was grave discontent among the masses, partly due perhaps to an economic recession in the fifth century (p. 29). Small farmers were constantly falling into debt. Under the Twelve Tables the debtor who would not or could not pay was liable in the end to be sold into slavery abroad by his creditor. No cases of this enslavement are even alleged in our tradition, but we hear much of a

---

[1] See J. A. Crook, *Law and Life of Rome*, London, Thames and Hudson (1967), ch. III, and (with some exaggerations), J. M. Kelly, *Roman Litigation*, Oxford, Clarendon Press (1966), chs. I–II.

mysterious contract called *nexum*, whereby the poor in return for loans had to work in bondage to the rich. We are told not only of frequent outcries against creditors, but of a persistent demand for distributions of land. Much land, it is said, was owned by the state (*ager publicus*) but exploited almost wholly by those who controlled the state, the patricians, for their own benefit. No doubt details in the stories of these agitations were invented in later ages when remission of debts and distribution of public land were again popular demands, but it is very unlikely that there is no truth at all in the tradition; indeed, in the fourth century, *nexum* was abolished, and it cannot be an anachronistic figment of the annalists' imagination. In addition, the consuls' jurisdiction over life and death seems to have been exercised in a harsh and arbitrary way; not only was it quite unchecked, but even the rules of the law and the forms of legal procedure were unpublished and known only to the priestly college of pontiffs, patricians who were also able to hold the great secular offices. The first successful agitation of the plebeians was, in fact, directed to securing greater protection for the common man against unjust force and chicanery.

In 494, according to the annalists, a great body of the plebs sat down *en masse* outside Rome and refused to serve in the army. Such a 'secession' or strike undoubtedly occurred in 287, and similar revolutionary action must have been taken now, to account for the concession the patricians were forced to make: this was the creation of the tribunate of the plebs. The ten tribunes were plebeians annually elected by an assembly organized in voting units, called tribes; these were local divisions of the state, originally four within the city and seventeen in the adjoining countryside. This assembly was truly democratic at the start, when the tribes were probably more or less equal in numbers; the rich had no superior voting power. The original function of the tribunes was to protect humble Romans against oppression by the magistrates; they did so by literally stepping between them and their intended victims (*intercessio*). The magistrates did not dare touch their persons, which were 'sacrosanct'; that meant that the

whole plebs were sworn to avenge them by lynching who-
ever laid hands on them. But their power was confined to
the city; outside the walls, Roman territory was still too
insecure for any restriction to be allowable on the discretion of the magistrates to act as they thought best for
the public safety. This limitation on tribunician power
subsisted throughout the Republic, long after its rationale
had disappeared.

As the leaders of the plebs the tribunes naturally sought
to aggrandize their authority in all sorts of ways.

They held meetings of the tribal assembly at which
resolutions they moved could be passed. These *plebiscita*
had at first no binding force for the whole state. They
could only be turned into laws by votes in the centuriate
assembly, and until 339 even the centuries could not
legislate without the sanction of the patrician senators.
Plebiscita were not finally given the force of laws until
287. The annalists indeed record that this innovation had
been made already both in 449 and 339, and many laws
earlier than 287 are said to have been introduced by
tribunes. There are many conjectural explanations of this
incoherence in the tradition, but we can be sure that,
whatever intermediate stages there may have been in the
development of the tribes' legislative power, it was not
fully established until 287, and that previously the con-
currence of the centuries or the patrician senators was
required. This made it easier for the patricians to impede
the popular will.

By the close of the struggle between the orders the
tribunes had turned their right of vetoing acts of oppression
committed by magistrates against individuals into one of
vetoing all official acts by magistrates, including legislative proposals, and even decrees of the Senate on which
the magistrates might act; this came to be the meaning of
intercessio. The tribunes could also veto each other's acts,
and one tribune could theoretically obstruct all the other
nine. This prerogative must have had a long evolution
which we cannot trace. It clearly stemmed from the fact
that the tribunes had popular might on their side.

The annalists also tell that in the early fifth century the

tribunes sought to try patricians for their lives before the tribes. There is probably a basis in fact for these stories, for the Twelve Tables enacted that only the centuriate assembly was competent to pass judgement on a citizen's life. The enactment is best explained as a prohibition of any future attempts to practise a sort of lynch law administered by the tribes.

It has indeed been connected with the supposed right of every citizen to appeal to the people against sentences of death and other severe punishments imposed by magistrates. This right of *provocatio* is alleged to have been granted or confirmed by laws of 509, 449 and 300; only the last is likely to have been historical, and that merely pronounced that violation of *provocatio* would be wicked, without prescribing any sanction. In the second century there was further legislation (p. 64), and on the orthodox view by that time all trials for grave crimes took place on appeal before the cumbrous centuriate assembly; moreover, the defendant could always evade the penalty by withdrawing from Roman jurisdiction and going into exile before the verdict was rendered; Tivoli (Tibur) and Palestrina (Praeneste) were conveniently near places of refuge. But it was never credible that a common crime, like murder, was tried in this way, and it has recently been argued that the procedure described really applied only to political cases, rather analogous to those dealt with in seventeenth-century England by impeachments or Acts of Attainder, that most common crimes were tried on private accusations by courts from which there was no appeal and which handed over the convicts to the vengeance of the accuser, and that the magistrates also retained the right to initiate proceedings and to execute inappellate sentences, if these had been passed by a judicial council they had enrolled.[1] However this may be, the citizen's right of appeal can never have been worth much, unless he could

---

[1] For a summary of this new hypothesis, advanced by W. Kunkel, see A. N. Sherwin-White, *Journal of Roman Studies*, 1964, 208 ff. Once Italy had been enfranchised, defendants could only escape from Roman jurisdiction by going to allied states overseas, and poor men must have lacked the means to do so.

count on the tribunes to enforce it, and they were unlikely to protect common malefactors.

It was only in the city that a tribune could ever person-ally intervene between a magistrate and a private citizen. However, tribunes acquired such political power that their views could not be neglected even where their writ did not run. A magistrate might fear that he could be brought to book by one of them after laying down office. By the third century the tribunes had obtained the right to prosecute political offenders before the centuries, and a breach of *provocatio* could attract such a prosecution. Breaches did occur, but they evoked intense indignation, and from time to time (as we shall see later) the protection of the citizen's person against magisterial tyranny once more became a subject of grave discord and popular agitation.

The first efforts of the tribunes were directed to obtaining greater legal equality; in 451–450 they secured the codi-fication and publication of the laws. 'When the laws are written down' said Euripides (*Supplices* 433 ff.) 'weak and rich men get equal justice; the weaker, when abused, can respond to the prosperous in kind, and the small man with justice on his side defeats the strong.' This result was not fully achieved in 451–450, nor indeed at any subsequent time at Rome. It was not enough that the substance of the laws was known, when the modes of legal procedure were still a secret of the pontiffs, and a litigant could be non-suited for using a single wrong word in a formula, e.g. substituting 'vine' for 'tree'. The procedural rules were not published till 304. Moreover, the substance of the law was still primitive and harsh; though it was to be gradually adapted to changing needs, not so much by new statutes as by adjustments made by the magistrates acting on the advice of lawyers and in virtue of their discretionary *imperium*, these adjustments were dictated mainly by the common interests of the upper class, to which their authors belonged, and the poor must always have found it hard to obtain redress. Hence the continuing importance of patronage (p. 49).

One rule in the Twelve Tables banned intermarriage between the orders, but was set aside after plebeian agitation in 445. Evidently there were now plebeians rich enough to entertain social ambitions and patricians ready to gratify them, perhaps in greed for handsome dowries. The intermixture of the orders inevitably undermined patrician exclusiveness in government too. In fact the demand followed at once that plebeians should be admitted to office. For reasons we do not know the patricians chose to meet it by suspending the consulship for most of the next eighty years and substituting a college of military tribunes (regimental officers) with consular powers; plebeians were eligible, but hardly any were elected in practice. This experience convinced the rich plebeians that their only course was to insist that at least one consulship each year should be closed to patricians. The concession was at last made in 366 after a long agitation led by the tribunes, Licinius and Sextius. It is said that they were re-elected for ten years and that for several they prevented the election of any other magistrates and impeded all public business. This is hard to believe, but it is likely that there was a period of virtual anarchy. Perhaps the right of the tribunes to veto all official acts, which is presupposed in the story as already recognized, actually developed out of a conflict in which they mobilized the masses against public order in a revolutionary way.

All the remaining offices were soon opened to plebeians, and in 300 they became eligible for the great priestly colleges, whose members often used their accredited knowledge of the divine will to obstruct obnoxious political measures. In 172 for the first time both consuls were plebeians, and thereafter this was common.

Licinius and Sextius can only have succeeded, where previous agitators had failed, in breaking down patrician opposition, because they linked the interests of the masses with those of their own small class. Ever since 450, if there is any truth in annalistic reports (as there surely must be), there had been an intermittent outcry for distribution of land and relief of debts, voiced no doubt when bad harvests or disastrous campaigns aggravated distress. Thousands of the poor were in fact settled in the territory of Veii (p. 3), but a few years later the Gallic sack of

Rome weakened her for a generation, the volume of debt grew and there was no more conquered land to share out. Licinius and Sextius are said to have promoted laws which provided for easy terms in repayment of loans and limited the amount of public land any single man could cultivate; probably too the law restricted the number of beasts he could pasture on uncultivated land. (There is no testimony that it was only now that plebeians were permitted to enjoy public land at all, and this modern conjecture seems to me implausible.) We do not know what the maxima fixed by the law of 367 were; the limit of 500 *iugera* of cultivable land, which existed in 133, is impossibly high in relation to the extent of Roman territory; it must have been raised later. There is probably good evidence of fines levied for transgressing the limit in 298, not to speak of a story that Licinius himself was fined on this account; this at least neatly illustrates the truth that there was no identity of economic interest between the masses and their political leaders, but only an alliance of temporary convenience, which was indispensable to the success of the political demands.

From 366 Rome was constantly enlarging her territory; the creation of ten new tribes between 358 and 241, in addition to the four already formed on the land of Veii, in newly conquered and settled territory, and the foundation of a score of Latin colonies in the same period, did much to assuage the demands for redistribution of land. The governing class could satisfy the land hunger of the poor without giving up any of their own possessions, and they themselves profited from the greater power which accrued to the city from the settlements (Chapter 1). But the landless still constituted about half the citizen population in the late third century (p. 13).

The burden of debt remained heavy. We hear from time to time of moratoria on payments or of the cancellation of interest due. The legal rate of interest was limited; eventually it was forbidden to charge interest. This law was still on the statute book in 89, when a praetor tried to enforce it. It had long been obsolete and perhaps had never been effective. It was not even to the advantage of those who needed loans; who would lend except to friends, with no chance of a return on his capital? In 326 *nexum* was abolished. Livy called this a new beginning of freedom. But perhaps its effect was not very great. Probably it meant that it was no longer permissible to lend on the basis that the debtor would become his creditor's bondsman automatically, if he failed to pay at the appointed time. Henceforth it was necessary to take the debtor to court. But if he could not or would not pay, the court would at all times authorize the creditor to hale him off in bonds to a private prison; in 216 many hundreds were released from this captivity to serve in the army. This put strong pressure on a man with assets he refused to realize, in the desire to keep them together for the benefit of his family; against the genuinely insolvent it served no purpose but vengeance. Debt was almost regarded as a crime, a concept still not remote from Cicero's mind. And a rational creditor, who might think it folly to imprison a debtor and maintain him with bare subsistence, might compel him to make an arrangement, whereby he worked off his debt. *Nexum* could thus revive under a new form. This was happening in 63 (p. 129), and perhaps some of the annalists' vivid descriptions of the debt-bondsmens' plight in the early Republic derive from what they had seen. As for debtors who had property and would not disgorge, by the late second century a new but harsh procedure had been devised under which all their assets could be sold up, and they themselves forfeited many of the rights of citizens.

The debt problem provoked the last great explosion in the struggle of the orders. It drove the plebs to secede once more in 287. Since a secession was only an effective weapon if carried out by the men liable to military service, it must have been the peasant proprietors who felt their livelihood to be in danger. A dictator named Quintus Hortensius (a plebeian) was appointed. We do not know what form of relief he found for the immediate grievances, but it must have been transitory. It was, however, of permanent importance that he passed the law under which the full legislative competence of the tribal assembly under tribunician presidency was at last conceded. Henceforth, most legislation was the work of the tribes and the tribunes. Rome now had more of the forms of democracy, but the vast size of the citizen body and the deferential character of society normally made them nugatory in practice.

Rome itself was becoming a large city. As censor in 312 Appius Claudius built the first aqueduct for its growing population; another was added by Manius Curius in 272. Appius also built the first great paved road, the Appian Road, from Rome to Capua, while Curius drained the Veline lake in Sabine country and settled thousands of Romans on the virgin soil. Appius was head of one of the greatest patrician houses, Curius a *parvenu*, but both seem to have been popular leaders; Curius, a heroic general and a model of old-time frugality, went about with an armed escort, terrifying the Senate, while it was a protégé of Appius who published the legal rules of procedure (p. 54). Their public works provided employment, like those of later 'demagogues'. Appius was perhaps the first to give votes to freedmen, but later censors minimized the effect of this by restricting them, irrespective of domicile, to the four city tribes; in these the votes of individuals counted least, precisely because they were the most populous. The controversy over the votes of freedmen shows that the number of slaves was markedly on the increase, a sinister sign for the future.

Dionysius of Halicarnassus stressed the moderation shown in the long struggle of the orders, which contrasted so sharply with the revolutionary bloodshed familiar in Greek cities. But what had been achieved? In form, a greater measure of democratic control: that was to prove an illusion. Plebeians had been admitted to office. But by giving up their monopoly, the patricians perpetuated for themselves a share in power. A new nobility arose to which only a few plebeians were admitted, and which was as dominant as the patricians had been. Its economic interests and oligarchic sentiments were no different. The order of society was basically unchanged. The old social conflicts were to re-appear, but it was harder for the poor to find champions, once the political ambitions of the rich plebeians had been satisfied. However, for nearly a century and a half Roman energies were mainly directed to conquests abroad, and the colonization that ensued from these conquests helped to assuage popular discontent.

4

The Era of Quiescence, 287–134

By 287 Rome had entered the world in which the Greeks were interested. The Arcadian statesman and historian, Polybius (*c.* 200–120), could draw on contemporary Greek accounts for the events of the third century and on his own knowledge thereafter; he lived for a long time at Rome and was an intimate of men in the governing circles, notably of Publius Cornelius Scipio Aemilianus (185–129), son of Lucius Aemilius Paullus, who conquered Macedonia (168), and himself the destroyer of Carthage (146) and of Spanish Numantia (133). Polybius also used the early Roman annals. The extensive remains of his huge work and the parts of Livy's history[1] that depend on it provide us with excellent evidence for Roman wars and diplomacy. But Polybius had little to say of internal developments. The annalists too, whose work underlies much of Livy and our other sources, concentrated on external affairs, and their accounts are still not free of inventions. Moreover, for many years neither Polybius' nor Livy's work survives, and we have to be content with much shorter accounts, especially those of two Greeks, Plutarch and Appian, who wrote in the second century AD. There is still little contemporary Roman literature. The treatise on agriculture and fragments of the speeches of Marcus Porcius Cato (234–149, consul 195) are of exceptional value; the comedies of Plautus (died 184) and Terence (died 159) contain much that illustrates social life, but it is often hard to distinguish between what they copied from Greek models and what derived from their own experience of Rome.

It is not surprising that our sources tell us relatively little of internal affairs. The wars, at any rate those with Carthage, were of epic grandeur, and their consequences in giving Rome dominance over the Mediterranean im-

[1] Extant for the years 218–168.

mediately patent, whereas the social and economic effects, sketched earlier, were gradual and long concealed. Roman efforts were concentrated on the defeat of foreign enemies, and internal conflicts were rare. Sallust observed that the period of domestic strife began when the fear of Carthage had been removed; that was not till its destruction in 146, for though Carthage had presented no real danger since 200, the sufferings of the earlier wars were so deeply imprinted in Roman memories that they could hardly appreciate how weak Carthage had become. The annalists with some plausibility held that even in the early Republic it was normally in years of external peace that agitation broke out among the plebs. The era described in this chapter was thus on the whole marked by apparent tranquillity at home.

Some internal changes or struggles do indeed merit notice. After 241, when the number of the tribes had been raised to its final maximum of 35, but before 218 the centuriate assembly was slightly remodelled. Henceforth, there were 70, not 80, voting units in the first property class, two for each tribe, one of men over forty-six and one of men between seventeen and forty-six. As the total number of voting units was still 193, there was no longer a majority when these 70 units and the 18 of cavalry were all agreed; at least the voters in the second class still had to be consulted. It remained true, however, throughout the Republic that the centuriate assembly was always dominated by the well-to-do. This is easily forgotten. We may be apt to think of Marius, for instance, as merely the favourite of the poor. In fact he was backed by wealthy men outside the Senate, and but for their support he could never have been elected consul.

The tribal assembly was also changing in character. The ten tribes added since 358 were all more distant from Rome than those previously in existence, and some were very remote. At first their votes were probably controlled by the more substantial proprietors who could best bear the costs of travel. Some old tribes also received new territory far from Rome, Pollia, for instance, in Cisalpine Gaul; in these tribes the votes of residents in such distant regions must have been far outbalanced by those cast by men still domiciled in the old tribal areas near the city. But some old tribes never had large accretions of territory, or none before 90; they were so small that they may have become pocket boroughs for great families, all the more as the land round Rome was increasingly absorbed in great estates, worked by slaves. As the free peasants moved out, many into the city, they should have been re-registered in the tribes of their new domicile. We do not know how systematically the censors did this. In any event, within the five years that elapsed between one census and the next some tribesmen would have migrated to Rome from the country and not yet been placed on the roll of the urban tribes; even a few score might easily have given them preponderance at ill-attended meetings of the assembly over fellow-tribesmen who still lived in the country. In 133 Tiberius Gracchus, seeking re-election as tribune, courted the urban vote, when his supporters in the countryside were absent for the harvest. This would have had little purpose, if the urban dwellers had still controlled only 4 votes out of 35. Earlier, he had appealed to the peasantry, and they had come in to vote for him, but this was quite exceptional. The electoral lists were only revised once or twice, if at all, between 70 and 28 (no formal census was completed in those years), and it is certain that by then the tribal assembly was not representative of the whole citizen body but only of the urban population. Probably that had long been true.

By contrast, residents in Rome never dominated the centuriate assembly to which, on important occasions, the rich repaired from the most distant regions. It is only an extreme example of this that in 57, when the centuries passed a law recalling Cicero from exile, he could say that it had the enthusiastic assent of the whole of Italy. In 70 Cicero remarked on the immense concourse from all Italy present for the elections, games and census; it is an illegitimate inference that it was primarily the census that had brought them there, or that all citizens had to come to Rome to be registered; 900,000 men could not have been housed or fed there. He was thinking only of the men of substance whose opinion mattered in politics, and who probably voted regularly in elections.

As a result of these changes the centuriate assembly, which elected the higher magistrates, normally the most important function of the people, became marginally more democratic, while the once democratic tribal assembly gradually ceased to be representative, and came to consist of the urban poor, except on rare occasions. It could be swayed by popular agitators, but more usually it was probably controlled by the rich on whose largesses the proletariate must have depended. Outright bribery indeed became more and more common, and the growing frequency of laws to repress it testifies only to their lack of effect.

Throughout the third century the foundation of colonies did something, but not enough, to satisfy land hunger. In 232 the tribune, Gaius Flaminius, carried a measure for the distribution of land on the Adriatic coast which had been in Rome's possession for fifty years. Probably the upper classes had exploited it for their herds, and the Senate bitterly opposed the law. Flaminius was a persistent opponent of the Senate. He may also have done something to reduce the burden of debt (Festus 470, ed. Lindsay). It was characteristic of such a popular leader that he provided employment by building a circus in Rome and a great road connecting the city with Rimini and the new settlements; the modern counterparts of these works still bear his name.

Flaminius did not propose the foundation of new colonies, 'bastions of empire', but the scattered settlement of the poor in a frontier area where they would be harder to defend, and his measure may well have provoked the Gauls, whose own territory was adjacent and who may have feared further Roman land-grabbing, into a dangerous new irruption. This in turn led on to the conquest of Cisalpine Gaul, where new Roman and Latin colonies were established between 218 and 177; when more orderly conditions had been assured, the Senate itself promoted further scattered settlements of Romans and Latins in Emilia and Piedmont in 173. In the south as well extensive

63

tracts were confiscated from rebellious Italians after the Hannibalic war, and apart from the foundation of some colonies, mostly small, to protect the coast, lands were allotted to veterans in Samnium and Apulia. Probably over 50,000 small farms were thus created for Romans and Latins in the generation after 200. The ruling landowners thus provided for a high proportion of those who had suffered from the prolongation of military service and the consequent neglect of their own lands, while the confiscations both in the south and in Cisalpine Gaul left them enormous acreages to exploit for themselves. Moreover, heavy mortality during Hannibal's invasion had substantially diminished the number of citizens who required allotments. But so far as we know, agrarian settlement almost ceased after about 170, whereas conscription continued to have dire effects; hence the land hunger which Tiberius Gracchus sought to satisfy in 133, the origin of which must be found principally in the previous thirty-five years.

Polybius saw in Flaminius' land law the first step in the demoralization of the people; he was probably writing after 133 and looked on him as a prototype of Gracchus. Flaminius, like Gracchus, acted in defiance of the Senate. Tribunes now seldom behaved in this way. There was very little 'popular' legislation or resistance to senatorial government. We hear indeed of no less than three laws which somehow strengthened the citizens' protection against arbitrary punishment by magistrates. One of them forbade the flogging of citizen soldiers with rods; as a result, canes were used instead. Probably any right of citizens to appeal to the people against capital sentences was now extended to those imposed outside Rome, but it can never have applied to military offences—it is amply attested that generals retained the power to execute citizens under their command—nor to common crimes, and the only effective sanction for observance of the right still lay in the readiness of tribunes to enforce it or to punish its violation (p. 54). It was precisely within this period that the Senate set up extraordinary commissions to try citizens for their lives without appeal on various charges of conspiracy, notably for participating in a secret Bacchic cult which was held to be immoral (186); Tiberius Gracchus' followers were punished in this way in 132. It was something different when permanent courts were set up for particular offences by enactment of the people. The first was in 149; it was to try charges of extortion in the provinces, but Cicero says (*Brutus* 106) that others were created while Gaius Carbo (consul 120) was young, and it is an unlikely assumption that *all* the standing courts of Cicero's time, which dealt with murder, forgery, peculation, bribery and treason were first created by Sulla. Before 123 any court was manned exclusively by senators. There was also no appeal from their verdicts.

Towards the end of this period we find evidence of increased readiness by the tribunes to adopt a popular role. It was to the tribunes that men appealed against real or alleged inequity in the military levies, often in vain; but it is significant of the growing oppressiveness of conscription that in 151, 149 and 138 they actually impeded the levy.

Independent control by the assembly was limited not only by the facts that the presiding magistrates alone had any initiative and that their motions could be obstructed by vetoes or by priestly trickery but also by the absence of secret voting; the humble citizens cast their votes under the inspection of the men to whose power and patronage they were subjected. The ballot was introduced by tribunician laws, first for elections in 139 and then for trials in 137; treason was excepted down to 107, and not till 131 was the ballot brought in for legislation; secrecy was probably not effectively obtained until 119, when Marius as tribune made it harder for the upper-class 'keepers of the ballots' to see how they were cast. Cicero was to deplore innovations which made it easier for voters to approve mischievous measures (*Laws* III, 34).

Mysteriously, the second of these ballot laws received powerful backing from the leading noble of the day, Scipio Aemilianus. His career indeed strangely prefigured those of Marius and Pompey. In 148 and 135 the people, led by a tribune, insisted that he should be elected to the consulship, for which he was not legally qualified, and entrusted with the command against Carthage and Numantia respectively. Ordinarily the allocation of provinces was a matter for the consuls to decide between themselves by agreement or lot, while it was for the Senate to extend their commands beyond the usual year; Scipio had to be given two years to finish each of his tasks. Enraged by the incompetence of generals selected on the principle that each noble must have his turn, and the unnecessary prolongation of burdensome campaigns which this incompetence entailed, the assembly asserted its sovereign control; its right to do so was to be a 'popular' claim throughout the late Republic. But probably Scipio was more than a war hero: he courted the favour of the masses, and was accompanied into the forum by a claque of freedmen and other plebeians. His friend, Laelius, even proposed an agrarian bill, which may have partly anticipated that to be moved by Gracchus, but earned the nickname of 'Prudent' by withdrawing it in deference to senatorial objections. Scipio and his associates were in fact not consistent supporters of popular causes, and were soon to be found among Gracchus' opponents. Nor is it clear that the ballot laws substantially altered the character of Roman politics. Certainly, the same kind of men continued to secure office after voting had become secret, and Gracchus' agrarian bill, as great a blow as was ever struck against the prerogatives and interests of the ruling class, was passed before the ballot had been introduced for legislation. The ballot laws of 139 and 137 are mainly of interest, like the resistance to conscription, and the agitations on behalf of Scipio, because they indicate rising discontent with the government of the nobility and a new readiness on the part of tribunes to act as champions of the people.

For most of this period almost all the laws they had proposed had had the sanction of the Senate, which actually found it convenient to induce tribunes to initiate the new statutes it wished to pass. Tribunes were also employed to veto actions by magistrates which the Senate disapproved, or to prosecute before the centuries offenders who had earned its displeasure. Hardly anything was done by tribunes unless on the instigation of the Senate or of a powerful faction within it. Livy (X, 37) called them 'chattels of the nobility' in an earlier time, an anachronism that had now come true. They were allowed to attend meetings of the Senate; many were senators; some were nobles, and the rest were generally hangers-on of noble families.

The term 'noble' means literally 'notable'. It characterized not only the patricians but the descendants of plebeians who had held the consulship, dictatorship or consular tribunate, or perhaps rather all members of such families. The plebeian nobility now vied with the patricians, and often surpassed them. None equalled the patrician Cornelii, a clan with many branches, in the number of magistracies they attained, but whereas the Julii, Caesar's patrician clan, counted only 6 consuls between 366 and 49, the plebeian Fulvii had 17 and the plebeian Caecilii Metelli 18; two brothers of this house held the office in 143 and 142 and six of their sons in the next generation. Cicero scoffingly remarked that Lucius Domitius Ahenobarbus had been destined for the consulship since birth (*To Atticus* IV, 8a, 2); he duly attained it in 54. Such men, he says, when asleep, received honours from the people. The talent of an individual mattered little; among themselves the oligarchs prized equality; re-election was limited and finally forbidden, so that as many as possible could have their turn; incompetence was common. But wealth was essential; without it even patrician families languished in oblivion, like the branch of the Cornelian clan revived by Sulla. Here too the plebeians could match the patricians; the Licinii Crassi acquired the nickname Dives; and Marcus Livius Drusus, tribune in 91, was the richest man in Rome and claimed to be 'patron' of the Senate. Domitius' landed wealth has already been mentioned (p. 34).

The exclusiveness of the nobility must not be exaggerated. Old families were always dying out or disappearing through poverty; 'new men' had to take their place. In almost every decade more than one family produced its first consul, generally after holding the lower offices for

67

generations. It was much less common for any one to rise to the top whose family had not served such an apprenticeship; they were 'new men' in the full sense. Cicero was the first (in 63) for thirty years, and even he, though often slighted by the nobles, may ultimately have had their support. The elder Cato had similarly been allied with a patrician Valerius. Only Marius of these new men gained election against the more or less united wishes of the nobility. New men themselves founded noble lines. Cicero describes his son as 'most noble'. In his day Cato's great-grandson was one of the foremost leaders of the nobility.

The nobility and the Senate were divided by factions. It is now fashionable to argue from dubious inferences that these factions were often hereditary alliances of families. There is no explicit testimony to this for any period, and in the time we know best, that of Cicero, the theory manifestly breaks down. Friendships, which occasionally rested on genuine feeling, were indeed more usually political connections, but they were made, dissolved, and renewed with bewildering rapidity. Even families were not united, and in civil wars kinsmen took opposed sides. Marcus Brutus, whose father Pompey had killed, espoused his cause in 49; pardoned and promoted by Caesar, he assassinated him. His fellow conspirator, another ex-Pompeian whom Caesar had honoured, Gaius Cassius had two brothers who fought for Caesar. These examples might be endlessly multiplied. Brutus and Cassius no doubt acted for the interest of the Republic, as they saw it; others could be guided by personal advantage. In the quiet times of the second century too we may suppose that individuals rather than families were constantly combining and re-combining to promote their own and their friends' careers or fortunes or to encompass what they regarded as the good of the state. And mutual rivals and enemies would come together, as the Gracchi found, when the authority of the Senate and the interests of the nobility as a whole were threatened. For Sallust the nobility constituted a single faction whose cohesiveness gave it strength against the scattered and unorganized masses.

68

The new men did not form a faction of their own, but attached themselves to those in existence. Moreover, once they were established, they had as much interest as any one in upholding the existing order. They had arrived at high rank and they had been rich from the start; otherwise politics would have been barred to them. They came from the class known as Equites (horsemen), whose property qualified them to serve in the cavalry. The Equites were justly called the 'seed-bed' of the Senate. They were connected by marriage with senators, even with nobles; they dined with them; they enjoyed all the same intellectual and social pursuits; and in general their economic interests were identical.

The most important, the 'flower of the order' in Cicero's eyes, were the state contractors, or publicans. As yet they had not obtained the right to 'farm' the direct taxes of great provinces, that is to say, to collect the taxes themselves or to arrange for their collection and to pocket the proceeds in return for their guarantee to pay a fixed sum to the treasury. The quotas of grain and fruits levied in Sicily were indeed 'farmed', but the contracts were let out in the province, and Romans did not normally bid at the local auctions. The Roman publicans did, however, lease the rich Spanish mines from the state, and probably collected customs duties in Italy and elsewhere. They also contracted to deliver army supplies and to construct and repair public buildings. Contracts went to the most favourable bids at auctions held every five years by the censors; they could be modified by the Senate. It was a wise regulation that senators might not legally profit by participating in these contracts, which they controlled; we cannot tell if it was evaded; but the principals in the contracts, the publicans *par excellence*, were by definition non-senators. Large sums were at stake; a great many men had an interest in the companies, which had to remain in existence for the duration of the contract and might renew it after five years. They needed a rather elaborate organization; their head offices were at Rome, and their interests often impinged on public policy; they formed, therefore, ever-present pressure groups. In 169/8 the strictness of the

censors, Tiberius Sempronius Gracchus and Gaius Claudius, in letting contracts so infuriated the publicans that
they put up a tribune to impeach the censors, who barely
escaped. Their influence depended not only on their
wealth but on their rendering services to the state, many
of which would now be performed by civil servants.

Other Equites were engaged in 'business' of other kinds,
as bankers, moneylenders, traders. It has been customary
to lump them together with the publicans and call them
all business-men, in contrast to the official class of landowners in the Senate. Sometimes the Equites are thought
of as the moneyed men *par excellence*. Again, commercial
interests are supposed to have brought them into frequent
conflict with the Senate. None of this will do.

The equestrian property qualification in the late Republic was not high, 100,000 *denarii*. At 5% it would have
brought in 5,000 a year, but even an economical gentle-
man in Cicero's circles needed 25,000 (*Paradoxes of the
Stoics* 49). Naturally many Equites possessed far more than
the minimum; some were very rich. But almost all the
richest Romans of the Republic we can name were
senators.

On general grounds we must assume that wealth was
mainly in land, and that most Equites were, like the
senators, landowners. To say nothing of individuals, this
can be demonstrated for the publicans as a class. They had
to find security *in land* for the sums they owed the treasury.
For the Asian taxes alone after 123 they were liable for
probably 15 millions a year; to cover this sum, if not five
times as much (for a five-year contract), they had to
pledge enormous estates. Gnaeus Plancius, the most
eminent publican of Cicero's time, owned land in the
fertile inland district of Atina. Most other Equites were
probably, like Cicero's father, simple country gentlemen.
Overseas 'business' could be landowning. Atticus, Cicero's
friend, had vast estates in Epirus, and there are many other
instances. Others were money-lenders, but senators too
lent money and often had more to lend.

Senators were certainly not in the ordinary sense
traders, as some Equites were; that is to say, they did not

buy goods to sell again. A mysterious law of 218, which Flaminius alone backed in the Senate, forbade them to own ships of a greater tonnage than they needed to transport the produce of their own estates. On this Livy briefly observes (XXI 63): 'any form of gain was thought unfitting for the fathers.' As it stands, his comment is absurd; even senators, as the law recognized, had to market their produce and make a profit on it; in this restricted sense there is ample later evidence that they were in trade. And by the first century the interdict on their owning large ships was obsolete. Still, none is ever called a shipowner, trader or banker. These enterprises were not thought safe (p. 21), and we may doubt if the Equites engaged in them were usually the wealthiest or most influential of their order. Nor were trading interests identical with those of the publicans who collected customs dues on seaborne goods; in 59 there is record of a dispute between them.

The hypothesis that the equestrian order as a whole had common economic interests divergent from the senatorial is thus unsound, and attempts to show that they wished to change the foreign policy of the Senate for the sake of their trading profits, which there is no space to refute here, have all broken down; they are least plausible for the time before 90, when many or most of the Italian traders abroad were allies with no votes and limited influence. But the publicans' interests could clash both with those of the treasury, of which the Senate was the jealous guardian (except against its own members), and with those of the provincial tax-payers, whom it had a duty to protect. The severity of the censors of 169 illustrates the first type of conflict (p. 70); the second was more apt to occur after Gaius Gracchus entrusted the collection of the Asian tithe to the publicans, but in 168 the Senate had allegedly refused to lease mines in Macedonia to them, on the ground that if it did so, the natives would be oppressed. The publicans were the richest of the Equites, and they alone were organized; in many passages where Cicero speaks of the Equites, the context shows that he means the publicans. It is tempting, therefore, to ascribe conflicts between the orders simply to the incompatibility of the

71

publicans' interests with the requirements of public policy. But this may not be the whole story.

Polybius says that the 'people' were dependent on the Senate partly because almost all were engaged in the public contracts (even before 123), and these the Senate could review, partly because only senators could decide the most important civil and criminal cases in the courts. As the poor had no money to invest, and generally cannot afford to litigate, he must have meant by the 'people' those rich non-senators whom he met socially, i.e. the Equites. They were the men who did not like being called clients (p. 48). They wished to have the appearance, and surely still more the reality, of independence. This was what Gaius Gracchus secured to them by granting them rights of jurisdiction (p. 88). And it was the prolonged dispute over control of the courts (123–70) which did most to divide the orders. No doubt the Equites desired such control because it offered a means of applying pressure on the Senate in their own material interests, or rather those of the publicans. But, as Cicero says, their juridical rights also gave them a position of 'dignity' or 'splendour'. In an aristocratic society this was highly prized.

And that is not all. Undoubtedly some Equites like Atticus preferred a life of private tranquillity, or chose to enjoy the profits of contracting which were denied to senators. But others were ambitious for public careers. Had this not been so, the Senate could never have obtained all the new recruits it needed. As dictator, Sulla doubled the size of the Senate and increased the number of junior magistrates, by drawing on 'the best Equites'. The post-Sullan Senate was full of such men. But even after Sulla the exclusiveness of the nobility made it hard for them to advance far. Marius, backed by the Equites from whom he sprang, had risen to the consulship when this exclusiveness was subjected to bitter attacks. The resentment must have been there before, and it persisted. It was voiced by both Cicero and Sallust, senators of equestrian birth. The relation of the Equites to the nobility was not unlike that of the rich plebeians to the patricians before 366, and the ambitions some of them entertained were common to the

Italian gentry (p. 10), who indeed constituted a large part of the order, after the allies had been enfranchised. Thus political aspirations, as well as special economic interests, could bring them into opposition to the nobility at times and make them the allies of social reformers. But basically they had no sympathy with the poor. They were land-owners and creditors, not landless or debtors; they did not desire to subvert senatorial rule but to share in it, to advance in the social scale or at least to divide the prizes of government; above all they required that order and property rights should be upheld. In the great struggles that occupy the next century their conflict with the nobility fulfils a subsidiary role; yet in the outcome they were the true gainers. By the time of Augustus the old nobility had been all but extinguished, and their place was taken by new men from the equestrian order and, above all, from the municipal oligarchies.

5

Reform and Reaction, 133–79

ALL historians of early nineteenth-century England know
that the Catholics were emancipated before the first
Reform Act and that that Act did not give the vote to the
working classes, however they interpret these facts. In the
period we are now to consider matters of almost this
magnitude are dark to us. The exact order of events is
sometimes uncertain. The content of a complex law may
be summarized, or distorted, in a single sentence. The
sources frequently contradict each other. All this heightens
the subjectivity inevitable in all historical writing; there is
almost a difference of kind between an account of this
period and those of times for which the abundance of
material leads only to variations in selection and emphasis.
For the brief sketch that follows some of our uncertainties
do not matter, since they affect details which must be
ignored, but I cannot refrain from making statements of
fact which do not accord with all the evidence and which
others might challenge; I shall indicate which these are.

Often obscure to us, the period was well known in
antiquity. Livy recounted it in great detail, and as there
were full contemporary narratives, including the memoirs
of some of the leading actors, like Sulla, it can be assumed
that on all major matters, especially those of public knowledge such as the provisions of laws, his record was
accurate. But it survives only in meagre and unreliable
epitomes. Our fullest narratives are those of the late Greek
writers, Appian and Plutarch, and these are often jejune
and dependent on sources we cannot identify or evaluate
with confidence. It is small compensation that we now
have some documentary information on Rome's internal
history, for it consists of fragments of inscriptions, which
often raise more problems than they solve. Our earliest
witness is Cicero, who was born in 106, and who had not
only read detailed accounts lost to us but had conversed

with men who had seen or taken part in the transactions of the time, but his numerous allusions to them, though of great value, are sometimes enigmatic or coloured by his own conservative prejudices. His younger contemporary, Sallust (86–*c*. 34), also wrote monographs, still extant, on the Jugurthine war, and on the conspiracy of Catiline in 63, and a history, now lost except for a few fragments, covering the years 78–67.

A *parvenu* from the Sabine country, Sallust had been a turbulent tribune in 52 and had rendered undistinguished service to Caesar as dictator before he retired from politics with a blemished moral reputation to vent his spleen in writing history, which he was no longer able to make. Since he had taken the 'popular' side in politics himself, and since his admiration for Marius and Caesar is patent in his works, he has been accused of party prejudice. This view is mistaken. Sallust's story is coloured rather by a high moral tone, strange in a man of his past. He extolled the qualities by which the Romans had gained their dominion, their frugality and industry, their courage and discipline, their devotion to the gods and the state, their good faith and justice to allies and subjects; in the good old days they had been inspired by a passion for the true glory which 'virtue' deserved. But empire and riches had corrupted the ruling class with luxury and avarice, arrogance and personal ambition, a vice that was only 'nearer to virtue' than greed.

In a famous comparison between Cato and Caesar, whom he regarded as the two great men of his own time, while praising both for their high qualities, he says of Caesar that he 'longed to have for himself a great command, an army, a new war in which his virtue might shine' (*Catiline* 54); this was plainly ambition, and in Sallust's view ambition was with avarice one of the two major causes of Roman decadence. He makes it clear that Marius was tainted with the same fault. A fragment of his *Histories* (I, 12) exemplifies his own claim to stand above the parties: 'Once the fear of Carthage was removed and men had leisure to prosecute their rivalries, there were numerous disturbances, riots and finally civil wars broke out; a few powerful men, under whose influence the majority had fallen, under the honourable pretence of standing for the Senate or the common people sought personal power; they did not earn the name of good and bad citizens by their service to the state—all were alike corrupt; a man was held to be good in proportion to his riches and strength to do wrong, simply because he defended the *status quo*.' This trenchant denunciation of the conservatives, who claimed to be the *boni* (good men), with reason assigns the greater blame to those who constituted the government; but it does not conceal the self-interested motives of their opponents. Sallust often castigates the pride of the nobility, but writing in the 30s, when they had almost been displaced by 'new men', he says that whereas the latter had once been wont to surpass the nobility by 'virtue', they were now striving for commands and offices by 'thieving and brigandage'. All the political elements in contemporary Roman society are condemned with impartial and unrelieved gloom.

Sallust's moralizing is not much to modern taste, and his idealization of old Rome is grossly exaggerated, but his ascription of the fall of the Republic to avarice and ambition is no more than a succinct formulation of what can hardly be gainsaid. The 'avarice' of the ruling class was reflected in the misery and discontent of the masses, of which Sallust (unlike Cicero) was keenly aware, and it was in this context of discontent that the ambition of men such as Marius and Sulla, Pompey and Caesar, was to wreck the established order.

Sallust recognized too that the leaders on both sides were 'a few powerful men'. The revolution began only when 'men *from the nobility* were found to prefer true glory to wrongful dominance'. Tiberius and Gaius Sempronius Gracchus, to whom he alludes, the only politicians except Cato to whom he concedes purity of motive, though in his view they showed too little moderation in success, came from the highest social order; their father was the strict censor of 169 (p. 70), their mother the daughter of the great Scipio Africanus who had conquered Hannibal; Tiberius was son-in-law to Appius Claudius, head of a

76

powerful patrician house, and Gaius to Publius Crassus (consul 131), the richest Roman of his time. Both Appius and Crassus backed Tiberius' reforms; and Crassus' brother, who was consul during Tiberius' tribunate in 133, gave legal advice. Some scholars suppose that Tiberius aimed primarily at establishing the dominance of a family faction, but there is no trace of this view in our sources; they depict him as the true author of his own proposals, not as a squeaking puppet for Appius or others, while his enemies alleged that he had been alienated from the Senate by a private grudge and accused him of seeking *personal* tyranny. It would be naïve to think that Tiberius and his friends were indifferent to the popularity that any benefits conferred on the masses always tend to win, but it is far too cynical to hold that *all* reformers *must* act from self-interested motives alone, and we have no authentic information from which to read *Tiberius'* own mind. He had to rely on a few kinsmen because most of his own order were against him. Even his brother-in-law and cousin by adoption, Scipio Aemilianus, who was in Spain when he heard of his death, quoted a line of Homer:

'So perish all who may like him offend',

and returned to obstruct Gracchus' policy, just as his close friends had already persecuted Gracchus' followers. It is a fundamental misunderstanding of the crisis of 133 to explain it primarily in terms of factional feuds.

Tiberius was concerned by the impoverishment of the citizens and the growth of slave labour. Travelling through Roman territory on the Etrurian coast, he had been dismayed to see great estates cultivated only by slaves. In 133 recollections of servile risings in Italy in 198, 196 and 185 had been quickened by the formidable revolt which had for years been desolating Sicily and which it took a consul to suppress. Moreover, slaves could never be employed to fight for Rome, as even the proletarian free could in emergencies. And the steady reduction of peasants to landless labourers not only diminished the number of *assidui* (p. 11) but threatened the future propagation of the Italian stock; the indigent could not afford to marry or to

77

'rear' children; that is to say, such as were born were often exposed and either died or were brought up as slaves. Even the censor of 131, Quintus Metellus, one of Tiberius' opponents, shared his apprehensions of a decline in population. The absolute figures for Roman citizens registered by the censors were indeed higher than two generations before, but the trends were sinister. Tiberius, who had served in the army with distinction, made it clear that one of his objectives was the maintenance of Roman military power, and although he spoke with great emotion and probably with sincerity of the misery of the poor who had fought for their country, the interest of the state was probably uppermost in his mind; it was to this that he subordinated that of his own class. On the traditional view voiced by old Cato farmers made the best soldiers. As a traditionalist Tiberius sought to revive the peasantry, from whom the legions were recruited.

His plan was to distribute to the poor public land, of which large parts had simply been 'occupied' for exclusive cultivation by 'possessors' or were open to common pasturage. It seems likely to me that the right to graze their beasts on, or even to cultivate, such public land had been essential to small owners, if they were to make up the yield from their tiny private holdings to what the subsistence of a family required (p. 35). But by now most of the public land had come into the hands of the rich, and the limits prescribed by law on the amount they might occupy (500 *iugera*) and on the number of cattle they could pasture on unoccupied domain (p. 35) had fallen into desuetude. The possessors had come to regard occupied land as their own for purposes of dowries, mortgages and sales, and had built on it their villas and family tombs; the distinction between occupied and privately owned land had vanished in practice, and in their view it was expropriation if they were now dispossessed. But Tiberius proposed to allow them to retain no more than the 500 *iugera* prescribed by law, plus 250 for each son (or perhaps each of the first two sons); all holdings in excess were to be available for distribution in small allotments, perhaps up to a maximum of 30 *iugera*.

78

People poured in from the country to oppose and support the bill. The opponents must have been those who stood to lose. It is clearly attested that Tiberius' supporters were drawn mainly from the rural population; they may have been tenants who hoped to get land of their own, small owners who wished to provide for younger sons, or landless labourers resident in the towns. Doubtless some displaced peasants had drifted into Rome, for what casual employment they could find there. Certainly the size of the city was greatly increasing; early in the second century new docks and markets had been built, and it was necessary to more than double the water-supply by building the Marcian and Tepulan Aqueducts in 144–140 and 127; the first of these works was very costly, and must have required much labour; distress probably ensued from unemployment on its completion. Some such displaced peasants it must have been who put up placards all over the city encouraging Tiberius to make his proposal. But in 129 Scipio Aemilianus could taunt an urban crowd with their servile extraction; for them 'Italy was but a stepmother', and we may surmise that, as in Cicero's time, freedmen preponderated vastly over freeborn (p. 37), and they had no connection with the land. In general men long domiciled in the city had no taste or aptitude for farm work; in 63 Cicero was to appeal against Rullus' agrarian bill (p. 123) to their preference for city life with its doles and shows, and even before the state had begun to distribute free or cheap grain, the great houses must have supported poor clients; in 100 and 87 the city mob were attached to their patrons, and the clients of the nobility helped to kill Tiberius. It is a complete mistake to suppose that either Tiberius' or any later agrarian scheme was designed for or attracted the urbanized population, or that any of them failed simply because the beneficiaries were mostly unused to work in the fields.

The rich possessors put up another tribune, Marcus Octavius, to veto Tiberius' bill. After prolonged altercations, Tiberius agreed to take it to the Senate, whose consent he had neglected to obtain, as constitutional custom required; no doubt he had foreseen that consent would not be forthcoming, and it was not. As Octavius declined to withdraw his veto, Tiberius carried another bill to depose him. This was wholly unprecedented and destroyed one of the safeguards of the constitution. His enemies said that he had violated tribunician sacrosanctity and impaired the freedom of a tribune even to protect individual citizens. Yet Polybius had written (VI, 16) that a tribune should 'always do what the people thought fit and most of all aim at (compliance with) its will', and certainly no tribune is known to have thwarted the manifest will of the assembly as Octavius had tried to do. Tiberius' defence amounted to a claim that the people was sovereign and that the tribunes were its creatures (Plutarch, *Tiberius Gracchus* 15).

The agrarian bill was now passed, and a triumvirate appointed, consisting of Tiberius himself, his young brother Gaius and his father-in-law, Appius, to see that it was implemented. This commission had full power to survey the public land, to decide all disputes of title and to allocate parcels to the poor. Its composition was constitutionally anomalous; it was thought improper for the author of a law or his kin to be members of a commission established under his law. But no others could be trusted to ensure that the measure was really carried out.

Money was required to stock the new farms, and the Senate controlled the treasury; Tiberius had apparently neglected to provide in his law for adequate funds. But a windfall came his way. Attalus III, king of Pergamum in west Asia Minor, made Rome heir to his personal property and to his kingdom. Tiberius passed a law whereby the royal treasure was to be applied to stocking the farms, and reserving the right of the people to decide how the kingdom was to be administered. This was an intrusion into the senatorial domains of finance, foreign policy and defence; for acceptance of the legacy involved new commitments overseas, and in fact a serious revolt in the kingdom had to be quelled before Rome could take it over. The principle of democratic control was thus given the widest extension. In practice it meant that Tiberius was taking the decisions, and his enemies alleged that he intended to make himself 'king' or tyrant, and threatened him with prosecution when his year was over. To meet this threat, he sought re-election; he would cover himself for another year with tribunician sacrosanctity. But if for a second year, why not for more? Moreover, re-election to the higher offices was illegal, and it could be argued that it was at least constitutionally improper for the tribunate; it destroyed the principle of accountability. This gave new colour to the hostile allegations.

Tiberius' rural supporters had left Rome once the agrarian bill had passed, and as the elections were held at the time of the harvest, he could not count on their return. He tried to ingratiate himself with the urban proletariate —how we do not know. Some sources also credit him with proposals to reduce the period of military service and to transfer judicial rights from the Senate to the Equites, and I doubt if they can be mere inventions. For his own protection he surrounded himself with a guard said to have numbered 3,000. All this was of no avail. Many of his colleagues opposed his re-election, and while disputes were taking place in the assembly, the Senate met and was adjured to prevent a revolutionary coup, before it was too late. The consul, Mucius, refused to authorize an illegal resort to force, but a party of senators, led by the Chief Pontiff, Scipio Nasica, a cousin of Tiberius, rushed out with their retainers; the commons deferentially made way for them; Tiberius fled for his life but was clubbed to death, along with scores of his followers. (The exact circumstances in which this fracas occurred are variously recounted and were probably never ascertained accurately.) This was plain murder, but it was endorsed *ex post facto* by the consuls of 132, who put to death many more of Tiberius' supporters on the ground that they had been revolutionary conspirators; Scipio Nasica sat as a member of the court, instead of being placed in the dock, though he soon found it prudent to leave Italy.

The gravamen of the charge against Tiberius was his unconstitutional conduct; the Senate did not venture to attempt the repeal of the agrarian law, and the commission, whose composition changed as members died but to which the tribes always elected Gracchan partisans, continued its work. There were endless difficulties in completing the land survey and in deciding controversies on title. The problem was the more delicate because much domain land was in the hands of allied townships and individuals; rich Italian 'possessors' sought to protect their own interests by alleging officially in the name of the cities they controlled that it was a breach of treaties, or at least of allied 'rights' (probably derived merely from usage), if they were deprived of land in excess of the legal maximum. Their cause was espoused by Scipio Aemilianus; in 129 he somehow contrived to have the commission's jurisdiction transferred to one of the consuls, who promptly left for a province; the work was suspended. Scipio died suddenly soon afterwards, and his death was rumoured to be due to poison, perhaps administered by a Gracchan partisan or by his wife, the sister of the Gracchi; there was of course no evidence. It seems that the commission recovered their powers, perhaps in 128; and in any event they must by now have acquired much land to distribute. Probably they had to keep their hands off Italian possessions, and if it be a fact (which is less certain than some think) that Italians had no share in allotments, that may have been a reprisal for the intervention of the Italian magnates. Logically Tiberius Gracchus' concern in the maintenance of Roman military power should have made him just as solicitous for the allies as for citizens, and so on Appian's view he was; a denial of this by Cicero may well be testimony tainted by ill-will.

One of the commissioners, Marcus Fulvius Flaccus, the last of a great noble house to hold the consulship (in 125), hoped to induce the rich Italians to surrender their public land in return for political privileges; he proposed to give them the choice between the citizenship and a right of appeal against Roman magistrates. They are said to have welcomed the offer, but it was resisted by the Senate, and Flaccus went off to fight a war. The immediate result was the revolt of the Latin colony of Fregellae, which was easily and ruthlessly suppressed. It was probably now that the Senate decided to appease the ruling class in the Latin cities by conceding citizenship to those who had held local

82

offices. There was not as yet any overwhelming desire for the Roman citizenship among all the Italians, but the idea was gradually to ferment in their minds until it resulted in the disastrous explosion of 91. More far-sighted than his contemporaries, Gaius Gracchus determined to settle the question without any greater delay than he required to organize such extensive backing that even a measure which in itself had no attraction for any elements in Roman society might pass by his authority.

He became tribune in December 124. He had been elected only in the fourth place, probably because his enemies contrived to prevent many of his supporters from casting their votes; they could only shout for him from windows and rooftops. He at once became dominant in the state. His re-election could not be opposed, and he even put his own candidate, Gaius Fannius, into the consulship for 122. Even more eloquent than his brother, fertile in ideas and boundless in energy, he had learned from Tiberius' failure and owed his success to the perception that a reformer could not rely solely on the peasantry, but had to overcome the Senate by creating a coalition of other interests.

Tiberius' efforts to win over the urban plebs and the Equites had been unpremeditated and came too late; according to Velleius (II, 3, 2) 'the greater and better part of the Equites' (obviously landed gentry, who lost by his agrarian law) and 'the plebs untouched by Tiberius' wicked designs' had joined in lynching him; by the latter expression Velleius doubtless means much the same as Tacitus, when he speaks of the 'sound plebeians bound to the great houses' (*Histories* I, 4). Gaius sought perhaps to detach them from their patrons, certainly to set up the Equites with a share in government to balance the Senate. But to what end? That we shall never know. He must have hated the men who had perpetrated or condoned his brother's murder, but after ten years he was hardly dominated by personal resentment. He was too shrewd to suppose that in the Republic any body but the Senate could carry on the government. We have a clue to his thinking in his law on consular provinces; they were to be allocated by the Senate, which alone knew the needs, but in advance of the elections, so that the people could choose men to perform tasks defined in advance. But the Senate was to have no exclusive control of policy. His own conduct shows that he held that the assembly might properly intervene in any field by legislation a tribune could promote. Did he dream of being himself a Roman Pericles, guiding the Republic by his authority and holding office from year to year? If so, he over-estimated the constancy of the electorate. Or, as some anecdotes suggest, did he realize that the course he took doomed him to ultimate destruction, and was he content to leave behind him a great name, as the man who had effected many useful reforms and created a more balanced political structure? Perhaps it would be unwise to assume that he had any single, fixed purpose. He may have thought each of his measures defensible in its own right, while seeing that each contributed to the success of the rest, and to his own power.

Gaius' objectives are the more difficult to determine because there is no agreement about the order in which all of his measures were passed. In my view, all belong to 123, but I shall here merely group them by subject matter.

The extant fragments of a later agrarian law, of 111 (p. 91), show that Gaius passed a law that superseded his brother's on the public land. In the literary sources it is barely mentioned; this suggests that it introduced no new principle but merely incorporated amendments prompted by experience. Gaius did, however, found or propose the foundation of a few colonies; one at Capua certainly came to nothing (the existing tenants of the Campanian land were not disturbed by the Gracchan commission), but settlers were sent to Tarentum and Scylacium in the south, and elsewhere some of the Gracchan settlers may now have been organized in colonies with local powers of self-government. More important, a colony was established across the sea on the fertile site of Carthage, abandoned since its destruction in 146. Carthage had been a great commercial centre, but it seems doubtful whether the colony was intended to inherit that role; Appian says that it was approved because it was thought that there were

84

good crops to be had in Africa. According to Plutarch the Italian colonies were designed for the 'most respectable citizens', and at Carthage the allotments could reach a maximum of 200 *iugera*, which would have required more labour to cultivate than the family of a single colonist could supply. It may then seem that the colonies were not for subsistence farmers, but for men of substantial resources. But the conclusion is uncertain. As in earlier Italian colonies, extra large allotments could be given to a few colonists, to attract men capable of administering a new city; the average holding may have been much smaller. Plutarch's statement derives from anti-Gracchan propaganda, and the underlying truth may be that Gaius gave lands to the younger sons of farmers who had a moderate property of their own but insufficient to provide for several children. Gracchus' colonial schemes are best taken as an extension of his brother's policy of rehabilitating the peasantry. But the conception of settlement across the sea was a novelty, which was to be developed on a large scale only by Caesar and his successors.

Gaius also built roads which may have been beneficial to the Gracchan settlers. His enactments that boys under eighteen were not to be enlisted and that soldiers were be given their clothes free were also of advantage to the peasantry, who furnished the legionaries. The second law was evidently repealed after his death, for by Augustus' time the cost of clothing was again deducted from pay. No doubt it was claimed that public expenditure had to be cut.

It was idle to suppose that the urban poor at Rome could or would settle on the land. With little regular employment (p. 37), they can hardly have subsisted but for doles and perhaps sometimes rent-free accommodation from the great families. To relieve their misery, if not also to diminish their dependence on his political adversaries, Gaius provided that they should be entitled to monthly rations of grain at a fixed price, subsidized by the state; in accordance with Greek democratic principles, under which citizens were, like share-holders, all entitled to dividends from public funds, there was no means test, any

85

more than in our own welfare state. Still, the measure in practice benefited only the poor resident at Rome. It is nonsense to think it inconsistent with the Gracchan agararian policy. Perhaps the doles attracted into the city a few who could not make a decent living in the country, but men cannot live, even physically, on bread alone, and until 58 distributions were not free. To pay for rent, clothes and other food, the urban poor must often have continued to look to the great houses; Gaius had failed, as many incidents show, to make them fully independent.

We cannot tell how the fixed price, which is recorded, compared with the average market price, but it must have been significantly lower; Gaius' adversaries complained that he was exhausting the treasury. It was probably to limit expenditure in years of scarcity that he embarked on a programme of building granaries, in which could be stored the products of bumper harvests, bought cheap. Like his roads, these also provided new employment. But for the time being they too cost money. Gaius needed new revenues. His speeches, we are told, were those of a champion of the treasury. He instituted new port-dues, presumably in Italy, but in the main he had to look to the provinces. Now and later, benefits to the poor in Italy involved further exploitation of Rome's subjects overseas.

The treasury of the kingdom of Pergamum, now the province of 'Asia', had already furnished money for stocking the farms of the Gracchan settlers. The administration of the province had been determined in 129. It then became liable to tribute (Velleius II, 38, 5), on what system we do not know; a document generally dated to that year refers to a dispute between the city of Pergamum, which was immune from taxes, and publicans who may have been as yet concerned only with the collection of revenues from former crown lands, and not from the cities previously subject to the kings. It is certain that Gaius enacted that the revenues of Asia should be collected by Roman publicans under five-year contracts let at Rome; his law remained the basis of taxation in Asia until the dictatorship of Caesar. It seems fairly clear that cities hitherto exempt were now subjected to the payment of a tithe on produce. There were also port-dues and taxes on cattle, collected by different Roman companies. Asia was by far the richest of Rome's possessions, and no doubt the new system produced a much higher return than the old. In the absence of a civil service employment of publicans seemed necessary; it was common practice in antiquity, except when lump sums were levied on communities, who were apt to use publicans of their own to collect what they had to pay. All publicans were oppressive; in the Gospels even the little men in Galilee are classed with sinners; but there was a vast difference for the taxpayers between local residents, who could not be wholly unresponsive to the pressure of public opinion, and the distant Roman companies with vast resources and influence over the government. Gaius can hardly have been unaware of the injustice and misery he was promoting; in 168 the Senate had declined to lease the Macedonian mines to publicans, partly because of this risk.

But his measure not only made it possible to finance his social reforms; it should have won the support of the richer Equites, who could count on enormous profits from their legitimate percentage of the takings, as well as from illicit exactions. Nor was this the only way in which he solicited their favour. The court that tried charges of extortion brought against Roman magistrates and provincial governors was manned by senators (p. 65), and some recent trials had flagrantly shown that they were too venal or too partial to members of their own order to do justice. Gaius transferred the right to sit on this court to Equites. But this meant that the governors who were bound in duty to see that the publicans collected no more than they were entitled could be at the mercy of the class in which the publicans predominated (p. 69). It therefore aggravated the oppressiveness of the publican system. In 92 the equestrian court was actually to condemn and ruin an eminent consular of outstanding rectitude, Rutilius, who had checked their rapacity in Asia. So far as we know, this case is almost unique, but Cicero, though always a friend to the Equites, admitted in 70 that avaricious governors had had to toady to the publicans and that many had suffered for acting against the interests and wishes of the order (*Against Verres* II, 3, 94). Diodorus says much the same (XXXIV–XXXV, 2, 31), and he reflects the views of the contemporary Greek historian, Posidonius.

Some sources state in general terms that Gracchus transferred the 'courts' to the Equites, but Plutarch records a law dividing jurisdiction equally between senators and Equites, while the wretched Epitomator of Livy, who mentions no legislation on the courts, says that he enacted that 600 Equites should be added to the Senate. Certainly no such addition was made, but it has often been supposed that either Plutarch or the Epitomator has given us a project which Gracchus first put forward and later abandoned in favour of a law by which senators were excluded altogether from jurisdiction. But such a radical change of plan would have been the kind of biographical detail Plutarch would have relished and sought to explain. In my view Plutarch's account is broadly correct and underlies the garbled version of the Epitomator who confused the roll of members of the Senate with the roll of members of the courts; Livy of course must have been right. We have therefore to distinguish two measures; one which excluded senators from trying cases of extortion, where their partiality was proved, and one which gave Equites and senators an equal share in the roll of persons qualified to hear other civil and criminal cases. As it was the composition of the extortion court, and of other courts constituted later on the same model to try political offences, that gave rise to major controversy between Senate and Equites, the second of these measures was ignored by most of our authorities. None the less, it was of some consequence. In the past, as Polybius shows (p. 72), the Equites had had to defer to the Senate, because senators were *their* judges in the most important civil and criminal cases; to make the Equites truly independent, they had to be given a share in *all* jurisdiction, though it would not have been sensible or welcome to eliminate senators from the work entirely, seeing that they had the most experience and legal knowledge. That Gracchus was not merely concerned with cases of extortion, in which only senators could be defendants, is shown not only by Plutarch's statement that the aim of his jurisdictional reform was to make the senators less formidable to the common people and the Equites, but by Appian's testimony that he made Equites judges of *all* Romans and Italians.

These judiciary measures were not popular. One of them was carried by the majority of a single tribe out of thirty-five. The common people had little love for the Equites. That did not matter to Gaius. Varro was to say that his legislation was to make the state two-headed. A passionate man, he is said to have put it more dramatically by claiming that he had left a sword in the ribs of the Senate (Diodorus XXXVII, 9).

He was also determined to protect the common people against that one-sided exercise of justice by a senatorial court which had done to death his brother's followers. Probably it was his very first act to declare by law that no citizen should be tried for his life except by order of the people. That left it open for the people itself to set up permanent courts to try certain offences (like murder), which they did, but it brought to an end, at any rate in Italy, the system whereby magistrates could convict on the advice of a council of their own choice. To break the law, or even to propose a breach, was itself a capital offence, and as this was given retroactive effect, the surviving consul of 132 had to go into exile.

Gaius' last objective was to raise the Latins to citizenship and the other Italians to the Latin right. But he had to defer this proposal until 122, and then his influence broke. He was for long absent, organizing the colony at Carthage; his enrolment of Italians among the colonists stirred up jealousy, and superstitious fears were evoked by his selection of a site that had been formally cursed. At Rome his colleague, Marcus Livius Drusus, overtrumped him by insincere demagogy, proposing colonies that were probably never founded, and suggesting that the claims of the allies could be satisfied if they were given rights of appeal against Roman magistrates; if he moved a bill to this effect, it was not passed, for even Latins remained subject to the Roman rods as late as 51. Gaius' own *protégé* as consul, Fannius, turned against him and argued that if the citizenship were extended the inhabitants of Rome would be shoved out of their places at the shows and assemblies. The enfranchisement proposal was vetoed or defeated. Gaius stood once more for election; he no longer had any positive programme, unless it was now that he held out hopes to debtors that they 'need only pay what they were willing to' (Nonius 728). The persistence of the debt problem is interesting; a Cato, probably a Gracchan, proposed a law about this time to regulate interest rates). Probably Gaius desired only to be in a position to prevent his measures being undone. But hostile colleagues refused to recognize the votes cast for him and he was not returned. In 121 a bill was brought in to terminate the colonization at Carthage. Gracchus foolishly resorted to force in resisting it, but the consul, Opimius, was well prepared; he had foreign troops in the city, an unexampled occurrence. Both senators and Equites armed themselves and their servants to repress disorder. Gaius and Flaccus, the consul of 125, his faithful ally, were cut down, and Opimius arrested and executed (it is said) 3,000 of their followers.

In taking this action, flagrantly contradictory of Gaius' recent law, Opimius was fortified by the so-called 'last decree' of the Senate, which was now passed for the first time and directed the magistrates to ensure that the state came to no harm. This did not confer on them any new legal authority but indicated that the state was in danger and that they would be justified in acting on the principle that the highest law was the public safety, in disregard of statutes. Opimius was indeed brought to trial before the centuries but acquitted. The upper classes, even the Equites, could not forgive Gaius' assault on public order and accepted Opimius' defence that Gaius and his followers had been justly put to death.

This alliance of senators and Equites made it inopportune for the Senate to attempt to reverse Gracchus' judiciary legislation. But the colony at Carthage was annulled (though the settlers, probably few, who had actually gone out were not disturbed). The corn-law too was amended, to substitute moderate for extravagant 'largesse' (Cicero, *Offices* II, 72). I conjecture that the new distributions were somewhat like those under a law of 73, which went to only 40,000 recipients, and that in both cases free birth was made a condition of receipt; it is hard to see on what other basis the number could have been so limited in 73, it could have been argued that the support of indigent freedmen was the responsibility of their patrons (who had a good motive for binding them in this way to loyalty), and as the freedmen were mainly confined to four of the thirty-five tribes, one can understand that what at first sight would seem to have been an unpopular measure of retrenchment might easily have obtained a majority. (The date of this measure is in doubt.)

What of the agrarian settlement? We do not know how many received allotments from the Gracchan commission. The transmitted census figures show an increase in the number of registered citizens from 319,000 in 130 to 395,000 in 124, and it can plausibly be supposed both that there had been little settlement before 131, and that subsequent registrations were more complete as a consequence of the settlements. But the figure for 124 is suspect, and little reliance can be placed on this argument. In any case, however many settlers there were, we are told that the scheme failed.

Tiberius Gracchus had made the allotments inalienable. This rule was no doubt suggested by Greek theory and practice; some modern experience shows that it could have served |to protect smallholdings. In the reaction after Gaius' death the first step was to abolish the rule. The rich were then entitled to buy the settlers out. Next, a halt was called to distributions and the commission was disbanded. In return the possessors were again required to pay rent, and the proceeds were applied to 'distributions', perhaps simply to paying for the state subsidy on grain in Rome. Finally, even this rent was abolished; this measure could hardly have gone through the tribal assembly, if it involved suspending distributions in cash, especially as it was apparently passed in 111, a year in which the Senate was under heavy attack (p. 96), but the grain doles could have been kept up from other revenues. The last law mentioned by Appian seems to be that of which we have large fragments on bronze; it shows that all the once 'occupied' land, as well as the Gracchan allotments, now became private property; most remaining public land was reserved for open pasturage, which is not to say that the rich did not in time illegally enclose and cultivate it, if they saw fit. In Appian's view the total result was that the poor 'lost everything' and were reduced to unemployment. The shortage of *assidui* in 107 is significant (p. 141).

If the holdings of the Gracchan settlers were as large as 30 *iugera*, which should have been ample for subsistence, it would indeed be surprising if all of them failed. But other peasants not yet dispossessed in 133 and less generously provided with land were doubtless being ruined by the old causes (pp. 33 ff); in particular violent expropriation (as Appian and Sallust allege) was perhaps common. And all alike suffered from the persistence of conscription. There was an inherent contradiction in the Gracchan objective of increasing the number of Rome's peasant soldiers, when it was soldiering that did much to destroy the peasantry.

The agrarian problem, which the Gracchi failed to solve, did not disappear. It became more acute, as it took a new form, the demand for allotments from veterans, themselves drawn from the rural proletariate, a demand they had the power to enforce if their commanders were ready to give leadership. The Senate triumphed over the Gracchi with the sword, but the sword was to fall into other hands.

The Gracchi exposed all the divisive forces in Roman society, and their reforms and ruin set in train the events that culminated with the fall of the Republic. The poor did not forget them but made daily offerings at their graves. Cicero, who strongly disapproved of their conduct, was obliged to speak of them to the people with respect, and Sallust observed that the cruel victory of the nobility left them with more apprehension than power (*Jugurtha* 42). Despite earlier premonitions of discord (p. 65), it was the Gracchi who opened the great cleavage in politics which both Cicero and Sallust regarded as fundamental in the late Republic. The death of Tiberius and his whole policy as tribune, said Cicero, divided the people into two parts (*Republic* I, 31). Sallust constantly insists on the hostility of the plebs, which now means the poor, to the 'faction' of the 'nobility', the 'few' who dominated the Senate, and claimed to uphold its authority; at times he virtually identifies the faction with the Senate. These men tyrannized over the state; the plebs sought 'liberty', which seems to mean sometimes freedom from oppression, at others an effective share in political power. For Cicero the division is between the *populares*, men whose character or measures he often describes as seditious and by other opprobrious terms, and the *optimates* or *boni* (good men). The Gracchi are frequently called *populares*, and Gaius, he thought, most of all deserved that name.

In his speech for Sestius (96-105) Cicero describes the *populares* as those who wished their words and actions to gratify the 'multitude' and adds that 'the inclinations of the multitude or the interest of the people often diverges from the advantage of the state'. By contrast the optimates include the whole class from whom the Senate is recruited, the country gentry, the business men, even freedmen, every one 'not a criminal or perverse by nature or frenzied or *embarrassed in his private affairs*'; all are optimates who in politics fulfil the duty of serving the wishes, *interests* and opinions of the 'good *and prosperous*', i.e. those whose morals are as sound as their bank balances. Elsewhere indeed, playing on the ambiguity of the Latin *popularis*, which might mean acting for the good of the people rather than merely 'popular', Cicero could claim that true *populares*, like himself, stood for the very principles he here attributes to the optimates; this emptied the term of its technical sense. Not, of course, that we can accept the distinction Cicero draws in his speech for Sestius as impartial. He makes membership of the optimates far too extensive, and as he has imbued them with his own principles (pp. 124 ff.), which, as he complains at times, they often ignored, so he imputes to the *populares* a mere

93

demagogy they would have repudiated; naturally they too claimed to be acting in the interest of the state.

It is the actual application of the two 'party' names to particular men and measures that shows what differentiated them. The *populares* were apt, in defiance of the Senate, to propose distributions of land and grain, or relief of debtors, the optimates to resist in the name of property rights or public economy. Occasionally, indeed, for the political advantage of the Senate, optimates swallowed their objections and themselves sponsored such measures, as did Drusus in 91 and Cato in 62 (p. 132). It was the general principle that *populares* acted through the people (Livy, III, 39, 9), and an opponent of democracy can also be described as 'averse to popular views' (Cicero, *Republic* III, 47 f.). None of them claimed indeed that the people at Rome, as at Athens, should control all policy and even routine administration; but they all asserted the sovereign right of the people to decide any question that might be referred to it, and rejected the optimate claim that the prior sanction of the Senate was required. Hence, the grants of extraordinary powers by the Assembly to Pompey in 67 and 66 were 'popular measures' (Cicero, *Philippics* XI, 17 f.). On the former occasion, the tribune Gabinius threatened to treat a colleague as Tiberius Gracchus had treated Octavius. Not even a tribunician veto must stand in the way of the popular will. Moreover, ballot laws and possibly grain distributions were to make the people less subservient to the nobility, and the ordinary man was to be protected against arbitrary punishment by the magistrates. This was a great part of liberty to the *populares*; to the optimates liberty was their own freedom to participate in government without fear or favour; according to Scipio Aemilianus 'worth (*dignitas*) springs from integrity, office from worth, power (*imperium*) from office, and liberty from power' (Astin, *Scipio Aemilianus* p. 267). The optimates were certainly oligarchs: were *populares* democrats? Of course they too were senators and often nobles, and they did not demand continuous government by the assembly. But they did uphold the sovereign right of the assembly to decide any matter that might be put to it, without the sanction of the Senate. In that limited sense they were democrats in their professions, and if their professions and their practice did not correspond, that does not distinguish them from politicians of other ages to whom we do not refuse the labels they claim. Perhaps no *populares*, at least after the Gracchi, were sincere; perhaps all sought only to satisfy their ambition or that of their leader. But again their personal motives, which it may be hard to determine, are less significant than the real grievances and genuine discontents on which they could play.

Neither optimates nor *populares* were organized parties with a permanent life. At most times the Senate was still divided into factions, actuated by private feuds, competing for offices or disputing on transitory questions of the moment. But these factions tended to close ranks when the authority or interests of the whole order were imperilled. There was an optimate party only when there was a popular threat to senatorial control. *Populares* came forward only at intervals, generally to carry some particular measure. Parties of the kind familiar in a modern representative democracy, permanent associations whose purpose is to win elections and hold power for a period of years, in which (to use Lord Melbourne's phrase), they must 'hang together', whether to carry out an agreed policy or simply to cling to office, had no rationale at Rome, where in Senate and assembly alike voters enjoyed rights for life, and majorities were made up by men who concurred on a specific objective but had no need to commit themselves to acting together continuously. But it does not follow that we should set aside the judgement of both Cicero and Sallust, men experienced in the politics of their time, that the state was fundamentally divided into two parts; if this division was apparent only intermittently, that was because the commons could so seldom find leaders. Few members of the ruling class were ready to be reviled for levity and turbulence and to be called seditious agitators by their fellows or to hope for advancement of their careers from the fickle support of the masses.

The Equites had helped the Senate to destroy Gaius

95

Gracchus. The combination was soon dissolved. An ambitious prince in the vassal African kingdom of Numidia, Jugurtha, continually flouted the Senate's will and, in overcoming his local rival, massacred Italians who had taken part against him. Public indignation forced the Senate in 111 to undertake a war they had reason to think useless and conducted without energy; negotiations with the enemy provoked suspicions of bribery, and were followed in 110 by a shameful defeat. A commission set up by tribunician law and probably manned by Equites banished many eminent men, including the hated Opimius, for their alleged guilt in these transactions. The war lingered on, and a new man, Gaius Marius, was elected consul for 107 by the centuries in defiance of the nobility, and appointed to the command by the votes of the tribes. The darling of 'all the artisans and rustics whose hands furnished their only wealth and prosperity' (Sallust, *Jugurthine War* 73), he was of equestrian origin, and was backed by the Equites. Some think that they favoured annexations in Africa, to which the Senate was adverse, so that they might have new lands to exploit; there is no evidence for this view, and after his victory in 105 Marius did not add an acre to Roman territory. More probably, like the people in general, they were incensed by what they regarded, rightly or wrongly, as the venality and inefficiency of the nobility. Sallust, however, shows that the anti-senatorial leaders, including Marius, were aggrieved by oligarchical exclusiveness. 'This was the first time' he says 'that the arrogance of the nobility was countered.' Hugh Last concluded that it was the very essence of the 'popular' programme to open a career to talents.[1] Certainly throughout the late Republic the exclusiveness of the nobility alienated many of the upper class. But that did not suffice to make them *populares*. They had nothing against senatorial rule, if they could be given a full share in it. Many typically popular measures were contrary to their interests. No one is labelled *popularis* simply because he was a 'new man' himself or stood for the advancement of other 'new men'. The movement against

[1] *Cambridge Ancient History* IX, 138 f.

the nobility in the Jugurthine war was indeed popular because it involved appeal to the people against the Senate, and because the people vented its rancour on the enemies of the Gracchi.

It was not only in Africa that the nobility was displaying incompetence. In the north a series of generals provoked the wandering German tribes of the Cimbri and Teutones and incurred defeats at their hands, the last at Arausio (Orange) in 105, one of the gravest Rome ever sustained. The wrath of the people rose again. Several of the culprits were tried for treason and condemned by the Assembly. In 103 the tribune, Lucius Appuleius Saturninus, introduced a more rational procedure, setting up by law a new permanent court, manned by Equites, to hear charges of treason. His law was to be superseded by one that Sulla passed (in 81), which among other things forbade any general to march out of his province or make war on his own authority without the sanction of people or Senate; I conjecture that this clause was taken from Saturninus' measure and that it was originally designed to prevent repetitions of the misconduct that had led to such great disasters. The treason trials, and Saturninus' law, once more show the people under the guidance of the *populares* claiming sovereign control over the state.

Fear of the Germans was so intense that Marius was re-elected consul in 104 and given the northern command. For the time they vanished to other parts, but as the danger might soon recur, Marius was returned each year until he destroyed them in 102 and 101, and even then, acclaimed as the saviour of Rome, he was elected for a sixth time to hold office in 100. Each election was contrary to the laws and the spirit of the constitution (p. 45). The popular will had advanced a *parvenu* to a dignity far greater than any noble had attained. Dignity and influence were in fact all that Marius passionately wanted; the idea of making himself sole master of the state never occurred to him. He can hardly be said to have had a political programme, but he did also desire to reward his soldiers with land. There were precedents; thus Scipio's veterans had received allotments after the Hannibalic war.

97

To secure this objective, and perhaps also to obtain his sixth and quite unnecessary consulship, he allied himself with Saturninus, who also became tribune again in 100. Probably Saturninus had passed a law in 103 under which Marius' soldiers were to receive parcels of land in Africa. He may also have then liberalized the grain distributions, perhaps by simply reviving Gaius Gracchus' provisions. He now proposed new land distributions and colonies. The details are obscure, but it is clear that the beneficiaries were to be countryfolk, all or mostly veterans, including Italian allies to whom Marius had shown his favour by enfranchising a whole battalion on the field of battle; it looks as if all who took part in the colonies were to get the citizenship. The Senate resisted the proposal, and it was carried by sheer force; the city mob, which cared nothing for agrarian bills, sided with their patrons, despite Saturninus' corn law, but the old soldiers naturally had the better of the fighting. Violence rose to a new level; nothing of this kind had occurred in 133 or 123. Saturninus was an adept in its use, and it led him too far; he had a candidate for the consulship murdered (himself an old opponent of the Senate), and even Marius had to turn against him. The Senate passed the 'last decree' again; all the respectable elements in society appeared in arms with their retainers under the consuls' command, reduced Saturninus and his friends to surrender, and then without instructions lynched them. Marius and the *populares* were discredited, and Saturninus' colonies were never founded, nor apparently was any land distributed to the veterans. (Most scholars think that some had been settled in Numidia under the enactment of 103, but in my judgement this belief is neither supported by the evidence nor probable in itself.)

Since 107 proletarians had been enlisted in the legions (p. 14). Appian's account of the disturbances in 100 shows that they came from the rural population, and all the evidence from the next century proves that the normal recruiting areas were the country districts; in complimentary vein Cicero was to describe Caesar's veterans as 'rustics, yet the most gallant of men and best of citizens'

(*To his Friends* XI, 7, 1), but when they took arms against the Senate, as 'men from the fields, if indeed they are to be called men and not rather beasts' (*Philippics* VIII, 9), while Virgil noted that in the civil wars 'the labourers are taken, the fields untended' (*Georgics* I, 503). Owning little or no property, these rural proletarians must have been tenants or landless labourers, but their indigence was only marginally greater than many of the peasants who had previously been liable, and were still liable, to the call-up, and who were often ruined in the course of their military service, whatever possessions they had had at the beginning. The enlistment of proletarians does not in itself explain the proposal to settle veterans on the land; soldiers of the old style would have been hardly in less need of allotments after several years in the army. The new factor was not a significant increase in the nature of the need, but the exceptional influence of a general who was anxious to satisfy it, though in the end too inept to succeed.

Marius' critics in later times alleged that ambition had prompted him to enlist men of the class 'by which he was honoured and had grown great; to a man seeking dominance the fittest instruments were the most necessitous people, who have nothing to care for, as they have nothing of their own, who look on anything as honourable if it pays them' (Sallust, *Jugurtha* 86). In fact the danger that a general could make himself master of the state did not materialize with Marius but with Sulla, Pompey and Caesar, and it is unlikely that in making a rather small change in recruitment Marius had any sinister motives or even that they were ascribed to him by contemporaries. Moreover, the huge requirements for soldiers in the civil wars would have made the change inevitable in the long run. Marius had only accelerated a process, and the root cause of the soldiers' disloyalty to the Republic in later days was not his action, not even the ambition of his successors, but the failure of the governing class to do anything to attach to the Republican order the men whose arms were indispensable in war.

Political turmoil did not end with Saturninus' death,

99

but the subsequent events are peculiarly obscure; we know, for instance, almost nothing of an agrarian bill moved in 99 by a tribune, Titius; it was vetoed, and Titius himself punished in 98 for having a bust of Saturninus in his house. It looks as if unity was still preserved between the Senate and the Equites, but this was dissolved at latest in 92 by the iniquitous condemnation of Rutilius (p. 87), which led a strong party in the Senate to make a determined attack on equestrian jurisdiction and provoke a bitter conflict between the two orders. Its champion was Marcus Livius Drusus, son of Gaius Gracchus' old opponent, a man of high birth, immense wealth and ostentatious rectitude, who became tribune in December 92. Although he adopted popular methods, he was acting in the interest of the nobility; he for long had the support of a majority in the Senate and with characteristic vanity claimed to be the Senate's patron.

The content and purpose of Drusus' proposals are endlessly disputed. The unreliable Epitomator of Livy says that he sought to divide jurisdiction between the Senate and the Equites. In my view it was already divided, except indeed for the courts that mattered most, those which tried charges of extortion and treason. Our other sources tell with confirmatory details that he proposed to transfer jurisdiction entirely to senators but to enlarge the Senate, and I have no doubt that Livy agreed. The Roman permanent criminal courts were large—fifty jurors served in a trial for extortion—and, as there were now undoubtedly several in existence, a Senate of three hundred members, many of whom were absent at any given time on official business, could not provide enough men. Drusus, therefore, proposed to double the number. The new senators were necessarily to be drawn from the Equites. It might seem that such a change would have made little difference. But this is not so. Publicans could not sit in the Senate. Drusus' measure would have excluded from jurisdiction the very men who had brought about Rutilius' ruin. The composition of the equestrian order was in fact heterogenous, and Drusus could hope that those who were enrolled in the Senate, probably mere landed gentry, would soon come to share the outlook of their peers. Sulla was to enact what Drusus had designed, with the same objective in view. Drusus indeed had another proposal, to make equestrian jurors liable to penalties for taking bribes, from which by a curious quirk of the law they had been exempt; this measure must have been retroactive and naturally gave great offence. And if some Equites were attracted by the prospect of seats in the Senate, the order as a whole resented the loss of its class privilege.

The quarrel between the rich can have been of little concern to the poor. To woo their support, Drusus offered new distributions of grain and land, reckless of cost. Of his grain bill we have no details, but to provide land allotments he found it necessary to entrench on the allied holdings of public domain, which the Gracchan commission had not touched. In compensation, he offered Roman citizenship to the allies. He may have hoped that the new citizens would become faithful partisans of the nobility, to whom they would owe their elevation, in any future conflicts with Equites or plebs. To my mind, however, it is probable (though it can never be proven) that he sincerely wished to promote this momentous change for its own sake and not just as a move in the political game.

In 95 the consuls had passed a law under which investigations were held of charges that Italians had usurped citizen rights. Nothing, we are told, did so much to alienate the ruling class among the allied peoples and to bring on the Social war. The revolt in autumn 91, was plainly concerted; this points to careful organization and to preparations over some years. We can surmise that wise men at Rome had become conscious of the danger, among them Lucius Licinius Crassus, one of the authors of the law of 95, who was now Drusus' most powerful backer, and that they had come to see enfranchisement as the only alternative to a fearful explosion. The allied leaders were willing to give Rome one more chance of peaceful concessions. But enfranchisement was not popular with the masses at Rome, who doubtless were still moved by the apprehensions on which Fannius had played in 122 (p. 90); perhaps too in a hierarchic society every one liked to look down on others less privileged in the scale. Nor did all the nobility approve of a 'leap in the dark'. They were to try to limit the voting rights of new citizens in 88–87. The sources do not explain this attitude. Perhaps they doubted their ability to manage a much enlarged electorate, though in fact in elections of the next generation they were to retain their dominance; only when they had been decimated or ruined by wars and proscriptions, did the political ambitions of the allied magnates (p. 10) come to fruition. In 91 the consul, Lucius Marcius Philippus, whose twisting career reveals a total lack of principle, led a powerful opposition to Drusus within the Senate. Drusus could only carry his other measures by force, and his bill to extend the citizenship seems never to have come to the vote.

In trying to conciliate every one except the publicans, he ultimately alienated almost all. Many allies resented loss of their lands, holding no doubt that they were entitled to citizenship without surrender of anything else they prized. The judiciary bill affronted the Equites as an order and was unwelcome to senators (we may presume) who did not wish to share their dignity. The death of Crassus in September was a fatal blow. Perhaps the Senate was increasingly alarmed by unrest in Italy and the readier to fall back on an ancient Roman tradition that no concessions should be made to threats of force. Philippus persuaded it to quash Drusus' laws on the ground that they had been passed illegally, under powers it had acquired by a consular law of 98 (which could never be used except against measures that no longer had much public support). Drusus acquiesced; soon afterwards he was stabbed to death in public, and the murderer was never sought out. His death was the signal for allied revolt, and the Equites were able to have a court set up, manned from their own number, to convict many of his supporters on the implausible charge that they had treasonably stirred up the rebellion; their real crime was obviously the assault on equestrian prerogatives.

Italy had enjoyed internal peace for some four generations, and the horrors of the war that had broken out and of those that were to follow must have made all the greater impact. In 90 and 89 over 250,000 men were in arms. For once Rome had to call up the freeborn in the city of Rome for field service, and even to employ freedmen in garrisons. Losses in battle were heavy on both sides; the enormous figures in our sources, though incredible, show that the fighting was known to have been extremely bloody. Most of it took place in the central Apennines and regions to the south, but in the later civil wars the main theatres of operations shifted to the vicinity of Rome itself, Etruria and Cisalpine Gaul; in the end hardly any part of Italy was spared. Many towns were burned or sacked, and some did not recover. Cultivation was naturally limited, and the armies frequently cut down and consumed the crops that had been sown, as much because they needed the food as in order to deny it to the enemy. The economic loss was more widespread and probably more intense than in the Hannibalic war.

By 88 all the rebels had been crushed except for the Samnites and Lucanians in the south, though in the process Rome had had to grant citizenship to the loyal Italians, particularly the Latins. But Rome's difficulties were the opportunity of the ambitious king Mithridates of Pontus (in north-east Asia Minor); sorely provoked by the Romans, he overran the province of Asia, and in 87 was to invade Macedon and Greece; everywhere Italians were massacred, and there were hardly any troops to impede his advance. Thus Rome lost Asia, her most lucrative possession, in which great sums had been invested by the publicans. This aggravated the crisis of credit, always apt to occur in civil wars, when the prevailing insecurity made men recall loans and hoard money. In 89 a praetor had tried to enforce the obsolete law against the taking of interest; he was murdered by exasperated creditors in the forum, and no inquiry was held. It was imperative to send an army against Mithridates, and the consul of 88, Lucius Cornelius Sulla, who had won notable victories against the Italian rebels, was designated for the command. Old Marius, who had also come out of retirement to fight the Italians, coveted the honour for himself. He found an ally in a noble named Publius Sulpicius Rufus, who held the tribunate.

In granting citizenship to the loyal allies, the Senate had tried to nullify its political value by enrolling them all in a few tribes, which could always be outvoted. The Italians' anger at this is decisive proof of the value they set on the *political* rights of citizens. As an old friend of Drusus, Sulpicius perhaps sought to complete the task Drusus had vainly essayed, and only turned to Marius and even to the Equites, Drusus' most bitter antagonists, because of the negative policy of the Senate and consuls. Conceivably the Equites favoured the claims of the new citizens in order to remove the risk of new disorder, which would also have hampered Rome in fighting Mithridates. But the evidence is so meagre that no conjectures can be offered with confidence about the convolutions of factions at this time.

Sulpicius drove the consuls from the forum by force and then carried laws for redistributing the new citizens and transferring the eastern command to Marius. Sulla had withdrawn to his camp at Capua. There he let it be thought that if Marius and not he were sent east, a different army would be employed, and that his men would lose the rich spoils they had learned to expect from his ability and generosity. They clamoured that he should march on Rome, and, though deserted by all but one of his officers, who disapproved of such an unexampled coup, he did so. Marius and Sulpicius were defenceless; Sulla occupied the city, annulled Sulpicius' laws and proscribed his leading enemies; Sulpicius was hunted down and killed, Marius escaped.

Sulla had a case. There was no ground for holding that Sulpicius' laws, carried by force, represented the true will of the people, and they were certainly contrary to the will of the Senate. Sulla met force with greater force. But he had fatally exposed the truth that the state was at the mercy of a determined general with an army whose fidelity was won simply by the hope of gain. This was a new stage in the process of revolution. Already in the Social war Sulla had set out to win the affection of his troops by relaxing discipline and allowing them to pillage a rebel city. Throughout his subsequent career he never neglected to cement the affection of his soldiers. They were to receive enormous rewards in the east and, ultimately, land allotments in Italy; Sallust averred that to secure their loyalty he indulged them contrary to ancient custom in luxury and excessive liberalities (*Catiline* 11). Sulla's best pupil was Caesar, who applied the lessons to quite different aims.

Sulla was and ever remained an optimate, devoted to the supremacy of the Senate. In 88 he hastily enacted new constitutional safeguards for its power, so short-lived that we need not consider them. He then departed for the east, where in the next few years he defeated Mithridates and restored Roman power. In the meantime an enemy, Lucius Cornelius Cinna, had been returned as consul for 87, and promptly revived Sulpicius' proposals. The Senate resisted, and the forum ran with blood; Cinna relied on the new citizens, the optimates on the city mob, still attached to the great houses. Cinna was compelled to flee, and the Senate deprived him of his office. This was a further constitutional innovation, and appealing to the remaining troops in Campania, Cinna represented it with reason as a breach of popular sovereignty; it did not lie with the Senate to take away what the people had given. More important, he could call on the resources of the cities newly enfranchised. Joined by Marius, he was able to mobilize forces which virtually starved Rome out. The victors entered the city, and proscribed the leading senators; some of Rome's most eminent men were put to death. Marius received the eastern command, but died before he could take it up.

For the years 86-84 Cinna and his friends were in control of Italy. They had professed popular sentiments, but, once in control, they paid small attention to popular rights. They had espoused the cause of the new citizens, and in the turmoil of 87 they, or the Senate, had promised the citizenship even to the defeated rebels and to the

Samnites and Lucanians, who had never laid their arms down, but it is doubtful if they took effective steps to see that the Italians were placed on the voting rolls. They had no policy and no principles. The crisis of credit had become graver; even the publicans were probably bank-rupted by losses in Asia; the treasury was bare; it was necessary to scale down public and private debts by three quarters. But it did not occur to the Marians to seek the allegiance either of the many who must have been ruined in the fighting or of the still larger class who had been in need before, by new measures of land settlement.

In 83 Sulla returned, resolved on vengeance. He had a well-trained but small army, only five legions. At the start his enemies heavily outnumbered him. But many of their troops had no heart for the war. Cinna had already been killed by the soldiers whom he had tried to take east, anticipating Sulla by an offensive. His successors were incompetent, and they had no cause to appeal to; Sulla soon made it clear that he did not intend to deprive the new citizens of their rights, and though some, especially in Etruria, Samnium and Lucania, did not trust his pledges, the Marians could no longer count on their united sup-port. Desertions began almost at once; when the soldiers' only motives for fighting, other than sheer compulsion, were either the hope of gain or personal loyalties, they were most apt to join the commander who had the best chance of winning (there would be no rewards for the conquered), or to take arms on behalf of their patrons. Sulla's victories in the east had given him initial prestige, and this was soon enhanced by new successes, while most survivors of the nobility, some of whom had had little choice but to feign acceptance of government by the murderers of their friends and kin, flocked to his standards. In Picenum Gnaeus Pompeius (106–48) raised three legions for Sulla; he had inherited great estates and numerous clients there from his father, consul in 89. Often the attitude of the local governments must have determined who fought for whom; they would conscribe soldiers for one side or the other. By the winter of 83/2 Sulla controlled large parts of Italy and was as well able as his enemies to 'collect troops by friendship, fear, money and promises' (Appian, *Civil Wars* I, 86). Another summer of heavy fighting ended the war. It was merely a struggle for power: no issue was at stake. But it left Sulla sole master of the state, and he used his dominance to reconstitute the political system in the interest of the oligarchy.

He had himself made dictator. The old six-monthly dictatorship had long fallen into abeyance, and Sulla did not revive it. He became dictator with no limit in time and with legislative power, though he chose to have his laws ratified by the people. Men spoke later of his *regnum* or tyranny. In all but name he was indeed king. But there was no possibility of his founding a dynasty; his only son was a child. Probably it did not occur to him to establish any other kind of monarchy. When he had finished his task, he retired; old and weary, he pined for sensual ease. Early in 78 he died suddenly. He had been free from fear of his enemies, having killed all who counted.

Marius and Cinna had executed a few of their principal opponents: Sulla's first step as dictator was systematically to proscribe over 2,000 men of note who had given any countenance to the Marians in the war. The victims were drawn from all parts of Italy, and his local partisans could often pay off private grudges; some were murdered first, condemned later. The sons of the proscribed were barred from office, their estates were confiscated. Communities which had taken the losing side suffered wholesale sequestrations of land, and some were deprived of citizenship. Samnium, where opposition had been strongest, was laid waste. Sulla hardly kept his promise to observe the rights of any new citizens, for no census was held until 69, and many probably remained unregistered in the tribes and centuries.

Sulla's aim was not only to punish his enemies but to reward his friends. By confiscating the property of the proscribed and of those who had died fighting against him, he vastly increased the public domain. Many Marians had themselves been great landowners. Sulla's partisans were allowed to buy up much of this property at knock-down prices; indeed some had not paid a penny years later. Naturally Sulla was the greatest profiteer of all. His acquisitions included slaves as well as land; he could even free over 10,000. Allotments were also granted to his soldiers, numbering 120,000 according to Appian, 80,000 on a more modest and realistic estimate. These land distributions must have been comparable to those effected by the Gracchi, and it has been argued that Sulla did as much as they had done to restore the peasantry. This is an illusion. Sulla wished to place his men in colonies in which several thousands could be kept together and rapidly mobilized to defend the new regime in case of need. For this purpose it was no use to him that so many great estates had been confiscated; they were widely scattered all over Italy, and went to his chief partisans; to concentrate his settlers in contiguous holdings, he seized whole tracts from Marian communities, expelling 'the innocent plebs' (Sallust, *Speech of Lepidus* 12); the colonists generally lived side by side with the small farmers they had expropriated, with feelings of reciprocal hatred.

Like the Gracchan settlers, Sulla's veterans too often failed to make good. The probable explanations will become clear later (pp. 129 f.). It was not because they were of urban origin or had lost the taste and aptitude for husbandry in prolonged military service. Their numbers show that three out of four must have joined his standards after he returned to Italy, and none were recruited in Rome, which he did not enter until 82. No doubt many had served in earlier campaigns, but they had not been continuously with the legions for years.

Sulla's constitutional design was to entrench the authority of the Senate against both plebs and Equites.

The plebs had no power, unless they could find leaders among the magistrates, generally the tribunes. Sulla limited the tribunician veto (just how we do not know) and deprived the tribunes of the right to initiate legislation, at any rate without the prior sanction of the Senate. Furthermore, no ex-tribune could henceforth hold any other office. Men of talent and ambition would hardly forego all chance of rising in the state. There should be no future Gracchi, no second Sulpicius. Tribunes of lowly rank would even be unlikely to stand up to the other magistrates against oppression of individuals, and the Sullan system was seen as an attack on the liberty and security of the common citizen. To Sulla it now seemed safe to assail in addition the material interests of the poor. He abolished the grain distributions and left the urban proletariate to such alleviations of their misery as the great houses might afford. The measure recoiled on the nobility, who could count less often after Sulla on the support of the city mob.

Probably Sulla hardly envisaged that the higher magistrates might be dangerous to the Senate. There had been no case in which both consuls had rejected its authority, and if one did so, the other would probably counteract him. Each of the eight praetors and two consuls would normally take one of the ten provinces after spending a year in Rome, and govern it for twelve months. In Spain, Transalpine and Cisalpine Gaul, Macedonia and Asia Minor there were more or less permanent garrisons, but they were too small to represent any danger to the home government, even if the governor were to hold command for more than a year and have time to win their affection. It is hard indeed to believe that Sulla could have supposed that commands would never be extended beyond a year—in practice such extensions proved common—or even that there would never be emergencies in which a larger force had to be concentrated under a general of exceptional ability, holding command for several years. Experience was to show that it was only in such circumstances that the Senate was exposed to pressure by an ambitious man who could count on the fidelity of his troops, and even then there was no danger from loyal optimates such as Quintus Metellus Pius (in Spain from 79 to 71) and Lucius Licinius Lucullus (in the East from 74 to 66). Sulla may well have thought that there was no risk of any one again behaving as he had done in 88 or 83 or Cinna in 87; the revolutionary conditions of those times could never be repeated. He had indeed only one conceivably effective mode of obviating such a risk, if it had occurred to him; that was to bind the troops to the government rather than to the general by providing that the state would pay them regular bounties on discharge. This was the course Augustus took, but it was costly; he had to impose death-duties on rich Italians to foot the bill. If the ruling class in the Republic had been prepared to pay for their 'liberty', they might have preserved it; instead, they had to contribute to the cost of a system under which that liberty was lost. At any rate Sulla did not regard the rewards liberally given to his own soldiers as a precedent; for the future legionaries were still to be discharged into destitution.

The Equites were deprived of their judicial rights, but not (as has sometimes been held) of their tax-farming contracts. As Drusus had seen, the Senate had to be enlarged to man the courts. Sulla recruited 'the best of the Equites' to make it five or six hundred strong; it was to be kept at that number by the automatic enrolment of twenty quaestors each year at the age of thirty or more. Sulla's new recruits, like the quaestors, were elected. He did not significantly touch the people's rights here; even the ballot laws were not repealed. The Senate became a less exclusive body. But the higher offices remained few; in general they were the perquisites of the nobility, who possessed the greatest wealth and patronage, and the Senate was dominated by those who had risen to them.

Sulla added one or two new permanent criminal courts and revised all the penal laws. No great new principles are apparent in this work, which has been absurdly overvalued by some modern scholars.

Cicero acknowledged that Sulla's cause in comparison with the Marian had been honourable, but in his view it was followed by a dishonourable victory. Once Sulla was dead, he had hardly a good word for him. He was a tyrant, 'a master of luxury, avarice and cruelty', and the time of his rule was calamitous. Perhaps Cicero was offended almost as much by his disregard for property rights as by his inhumanity. But his was the universal verdict of antiquity. The ancients judged Sulla by moral standards and condemned him: the moderns are kinder, because they are more prone to magnify success. Yet Sulla achieved little besides adding to the sum of human misery. His system soon crumbled; it aggrieved the Equites, the city mob, the dispossessed, the new citizens and failed to provide for the soldiery. What endured was the memory of his example and methods. In 49 Cicero depicts the Pompeians as thinking of the proscriptions and confiscations and saying to themselves: 'Sulla could do it; why not I?'. In 63 Catiline had had the same thoughts. For the next thirty years Italy feared a new Sulla. In marching on Rome and making himself dictator Caesar followed the precedents Sulla had set, but he won over public opinion by his well-advertised abhorrence of Sulla's cruelty.

6

The Fall of the Republic, 78–27

> *The good-will of the governed will be starved if it is not
> fed by the good conduct of the governors.*
> (Lord Halifax)

WE know far more of Roman history from about 65 to 40
than of any previous era. Documentary material is not
copious, but we now have much contemporary writing.
Of Sallust enough has been said (pp. 75 f.). The com-
mentaries on the Gallic and civil wars by Caesar (100–44)
and his continuators have little relevance to our subject,
but the works of Cicero (106–43), speeches, letters and
also treatises on rhetoric and philosophy which contain
many historical allusions, are of the highest value, though
they tell us too little of the conditions and desires of the
lower classes. Cicero's correspondence consists partly of
letters exchanged with his most eminent contemporaries,
but intimate revelations of his daily thoughts, in which
no attempt is made to conceal the truth, are found,
especially when he writes to a life-long equestrian friend,
Atticus, who moved in the highest circles but preserved
in politics a prudent neutrality. His speeches are another
matter. Some were delivered for private clients, and we
can seldom be sure (as we can with his defence of Sestius)
that he was expressing his own views. Even his political
orations are not always sincere. In both there are dis-
tortions or omissions to fit his case. His genuine opinions
come out in his theoretical treatises as well as in his
letters.

Down to about 65 evidence remains meagre, and even
thereafter the gaps in contemporary testimony are considerable and leave many problems unsolved. As the great
histories of Sallust, Pollio (consul in 40) and Livy are lost,
a continuous narrative still rests on late accounts whose

112

sources are unknown. Cassius Dio, who held high office in the early third century AD, supplies the best framework from 67; he sought to pierce the surface of events, but did not always understand the Republican setting. Appian and Plutarch remain important; the former's story of events from Caesar's death to 35 is the fullest we have, and its details are often confirmed by Cicero; probably he drew ultimately on Pollio. Suetonius' lives of Caesar and Augustus, written in the early second century, mingle dubious anecdotes with valuable information. There is of course scattered evidence elsewhere. Varro (116–27) gives us a picture of the great estates in his work on rural economy.

Sulla was scarcely in his grave when discontent broke out into violence. In Etruria the dispossessed peasants attacked his settlers. Under pretence of restoring order, the consul of 78, Marcus Aemilius Lepidus, raised a formidable army and called for the re-institution of grain doles (this was temporarily conceded), the restoration of tribunician power, the restitution to Italian communities of citizen rights which Sulla had purported to take away (that was effected through the courts) and, above all, a new deal on the land. Lepidus claimed that veterans had been fobbed off with 'woods and marshes' (perhaps with some truth), that all the best land had gone to a few of Sulla's favourites and that by a more equitable distribution every one could be satisfied, Sulla's soldiers as well as the dispossessed. His own past record was tainted, and his ability modest; yet a system which left almost every one embittered was so vulnerable that he could raise a revolt which was suppressed only with difficulty in 77. Apparently the veterans did not trust him, and rallied to the Senate, as Sulla had hoped.

An essential part in his defeat was played by young Pompey, who was again called on to raise and command an army, though he held no official position. Now and in the next few years the Senate was handicapped by a dearth of talent; nearly all its experienced members' and no doubt many younger men of promise too, had perished in the civil wars and proscriptions. In Spain, a brilliant Marian officer, Quintus Sertorius, had already raised a rebellion, depending almost wholly on natives who doubtless wished to shake off Roman rule; since 79 Quintus Metellus had been trying to subdue it without much success. Now Sertorius was reinforced by the remnants of Lepidus' army, some 20,000 men. It was necessary to reinforce Metellus, and the Senate had little choice but to despatch Pompey. For the third time he was entrusted with an extraordinary command. He and Metellus only reduced Spain to submission in 71.

Pompey's remarkable achievements inspired him with an inordinate ambition that was to be fatal to the Republic. He had a gift for organization; never truly happy save when active as general and administrator, at once serving the state and amassing patronage, profits and power, he sought a succession of high commands. This denied opportunities to his peers and conflicted with the oligarchs' hankering for equality within their own limited class. It also aroused suspicion that he aimed at the autocratic power Sulla had held. That was unjustified, yet Pompey thought himself entitled to be recognized as the first man at Rome, and though he probably wished above all to secure this recognition from his own class, the nobility, he loved applause and courted popularity, and was ready enough to take from the people what the Senate would not willingly grant. He was not, therefore, loyal to the optimates, who feared him for his ill-concealed ambition, violent past and unscrupulous political manœuvres. The cleft that opened between him and the Senate led him in 70 to subvert the Sullan system and in 59 to promote the career of Caesar, who was to destroy him. But for Pompey's friendship Caesar would have had no opportunity to conquer Gaul, but for his later enmity no pretext to make himself master of the state.

Fighting in these years was not confined to Spain. To say nothing of border campaigns in Macedon, in 74 a great war broke out in the east, once more against Mithridates, and large forces were kept there until 62. In 73 a slave revolt in Italy, led by Spartacus, attained such proportions that by 71 ten legions were needed to suppress it.

Probably nearly 200,000 Italians, more than one in six of the free adult males, were under arms in the various campaigns at this time.

Spartacus did not lead a protest movement against slavery, still less a rising of the whole proletariate; few free men would collaborate with the slaves. Most of his followers seem to have come from peoples beyond the Alps; they simply wanted to escape home to freedom. But they were easily diverted by plunder, and had no choice but to live off the country. They may have numbered up to 150,000. Their devastations extended from Cisalpine Gaul to the extreme south. Most of them were killed fighting or put to death on capture; some probably took refuge in the hills. Naturally their owners suffered severe economic loss. Until they could obtain replacements, the demand for free labour on the great estates must have gone up. But small farmers probably suffered most, as they had no reserves to tide them over when their stores were plundered, their crops or trees destroyed and their houses burned down. Moreover, large numbers must have been called up into the legions.

The risings of Lepidus and Spartacus revived on a smaller scale the miseries caused by the civil wars, which were repeated in 43–40. In 66 Cicero could appeal to the recollection of Italians that 'when hostile forces are near, even if no actual incursion has taken place, herds are deserted, cultivation of the soil is abandoned, the merchants' ships lie idle in port' (*For the Manilian Law* 15). Roman armies themselves inflicted serious damage. Cicero claimed that abroad they ruined as many friendly cities on whom they were quartered for the winter as they destroyed enemy cities, and for verification he appealed to memories of their marches in Italy. The jurist, Labeo, probably with wars of the 40s in mind, put the case that a tenant fled on the mere approach of the soldiers, who occupied his house and removed the window-frames, etc, presumably for firewood; was the liability on owner or tenant? In 43 Decimus Brutus, about to stand a siege in Modena (Mutina), killed and salted all the cattle for meat, and Antony, marching from Brindisi to attack him, emptied storehouses and slaughtered cattle *en route*. Sulla for a time and Caesar with incomplete success tried to hold their men in check, but such incidents, or worse, must have been familiar, whenever Italy was the scene of military operations.

At other times too violence was now endemic. The decade of civil war had habituated men to it. Forcible expropriation was more common. Even men of substance might find their slaves killed and their property seized by armed gangs maintained by a neighbour. In 73 a new and sterner procedure was introduced by which fourfold damages could be obtained for such attacks. Other remedies against force or terrorism were probably devised about this time. One may doubt how effective they were, particularly to safeguard the poor. Small farmers were obviously most vulnerable to the violence practised by influential neighbours with large slave households, and had less chance of speedy redress in the courts, if indeed they could get any. They could hardly secure the services of a Cicero as advocate.[1] One way of extending your acreage was simply to tear up boundary marks; the practice was of course forbidden, but persisted.

Danger also beset men's lives and freedom. A century later it was remarked as a peculiarity of Cicero's age that gentlemen did not travel outside Rome without an armed escort. Highwaymen were abroad who would seize the defenceless traveller and sell him into slavery, if they did not simply despoil and kill him. Many were perhaps persons who had been ruined in the wars or had escaped from the bands of Spartacus and, later, of Catiline. Those they kidnapped might find themselves in the prisons (*ergastula*) in which great landowners kept their slaves in chains; they had little chance of emerging from these remote rural fastnesses to vindicate their freedom in the courts. In these prisons many who had been captured in the Social and civil wars may also have lingered out a wretched life. There was indeed a criminal law, probably of this period, against kidnapping, and a civil process whereby you could be required to produce a free man

[1] His speeches for Caecina and Tullius afford much evidence.

whom you were illegally detaining; but how could his friends ascertain the whereabouts of such a man? The numerous legal allusions, one as early as 204, to 'a free man kept in good faith as a slave' are sinister, suggesting that free men were often bought by those who did not know their status (or took good care not to ask awkward questions). Brigandage was most common in the pastoral uplands, on the cattle-tracks and in the mountain forests. In 60 the Senate designated these as the province in which the consuls of 59 were to restore order. The intention was to deprive Caesar, who was certain to be elected, of a great command. But there was a real need for special measures, and in 36 Augustus appointed a man of consular rank to do the job Caesar had understandably scorned.

These conditions made it hard to sustain the oligarchs' claim that the Sullan system had to be preserved in the interest of order (*otium*). Its opponents could reply that the Sullan order was in any case equivalent to 'servitude' and that the liberty of the citizens depended on the restoration of the tribunician power. They alleged that in the countryside citizens were not safe from beatings and executions by magistrates (Sallust, *Speech of Macer* 26 f.). In the city tribunes could still intervene on behalf of an individual who was suffering wrong, but their writ did not run beyond its boundaries, and it may be that Sulla had removed their power to impeach former magistrates before the centuries, perhaps the only effective restraint on disregard of citizen rights outside Rome. An agitation to repeal Sulla's legislation on the tribunician power had begun in 78, and in 75 a consul, Gaius Aurelius Cotta, found it prudent to pass a law relieving tribunes of their disqualification for higher offices; this gave them no additional power and merely intensified the agitation, since more ambitious men were now ready to hold the tribunate. But the tribunate had first gained its powers as a result of 'secessions' or military strikes; now the masses were too scattered and unorganized to exert overwhelming pressure; the effective popular instrument was the army.

Pompey returned in 71 and chose not to disband his forces until his triumph at the end of the year. The privilege he sought for himself of election to the consulship below the prescribed age and without his having held any qualifying office could in any event not have been withheld; but he menaced the oligarchy with other demands. He openly approved of restoring the old tribunician rights, and inveighed against misgovernment in the provinces and corruption in the senatorial courts. He was perhaps displeased with the Senate for having afforded him inadequate supplies in Spain, and he appears always to have stood for efficient government, when that did not conflict with his own personal interests. Efficiency had been sadly lacking in the last few years, and Pompey's influence was now likely to be enhanced if he stood for popular reforms. The venality of many senatorial jurors had aroused general opprobrium; a leading optimate could say that but for this there would not have been such pressure for restoring tribunician power; it also gave rise to the demand that censors should be appointed to purge the Senate, though the censorship was not usually a popular institution. Even the masses occasionally showed some interest in justice and good government.

The story of Pompey's first consulship and of the next few years is ill-documented, and much remains mysterious. He was saddled with Marcus Licinius Crassus as a colleague. The scion of a great noble house, Crassus had suppressed the slave rising; from profits in the Sullan auctions he had built up a fortune which exceeded that of any other Roman, until the spoils of conquests made Pompey and Caesar still richer; he was expert in underhand intrigue; and he devoted his career largely to frustrating Pompey, often under the cover of collaborating with him. Together, they carried a law to repeal Sulla's limitations on the power of tribunes. Censors were elected and eliminated sixty four men from the roll of the Senate; they also held the first tolerably complete census since 90, and at last gave many of the new citizens effective rights. Then Pompey and Crassus quarrelled openly, and could do nothing more. It was left to a praetor, Aurelius, late in the year to revise the composition of the courts.

His law provided that they should be manned from three panels, composed of senators, Equites and *tribuni aerarii* respectively. The second panel was clearly composed of those who had the distinction, conferred or taken away by the censors, of possessing a horse at public cost. The *tribuni aerarii* were holders of an obsolete and sinecure post, and may also have been enrolled by the censors. As Cicero classes them too as members of the equestrian order (*For Flaccus* 4), it looks as if they had the equestrian census; in a broad sense of the term Equites outnumbered senators in the courts by two to one. I conjecture that these rather artificial qualifications for jury service were preferred to a simple property qualification on the plea that the integrity of the courts could be upheld by the moral control the censors could exercise. In fact corruption remained as great an evil as ever. What the law did was to end the old struggle between Senate and Equites for judiciary control. The Senate had no opportunity to repeal Aurelius' law, and little motive; in a few trials we know how jurors of the different panels voted, and the voting was not on class lines. Henceforth there was seldom any clash of interests between Senate and Equites, and it was realistic for Cicero to urge that the orders should act in harmony.

The masses gained little from these changes, except that the tribunes could now afford them more personal protection. Even the soldiers were cheated of rewards. Probably in 70 a tribune, Plotius, promoted a law whereby the veterans of the Sertorian war were to receive land allotments; in 59 it had still not been carried out. As after his return from the East in 62, Pompey evidently showed no aptitude for putting into effect what he must have desired. Nor were the corn distributions fully revived. In 75 there had been a 'cruel' scarcity; the consuls had been assaulted by a hungry mob on Rome's principal thoroughfare, the Via Sacra. Their successors in 73 had been obliged to introduce distributions, probably at the

Gracchan price, but restricted to 40,000 recipients. Perhaps four fifths of the free urban poor were excluded. I have already conjectured (p. 91) that only the freeborn were to benefit.

Even after 70 few tribunes appeared as champions of the masses. Sallust depicts the tribune, Licinius Macer, in 73 stressing his difficulty in assailing the resources of the nobility 'alone, powerless, a magistrate only in name' (*Speech of Macer* 3). The tribunate had since recovered its old rights, but its holders were doubtless still apt to think of their future political prospects; they were either nobles or dependent on noble backing. The popular tribunes themselves mostly relied on great figures such as Pompey or Caesar and were their instruments; only Clodius stands apart. But the populace could achieve nothing without leadership.

Distress at Rome had for years been aggravated by the activities of the pirates. Centred in Cilicia, they had equipped great fleets and, as Rome had no navy, controlled the seas. The Senate had taken piecemeal measures against them without result. It had become unsafe to sail except in the winter, the very season when ancient navigators normally dared not leave port. The transport of troops and of public moneys was endangered, still more the grain convoys on which the Roman populace depended for bread. The depredations extended to harbours and the interior; a fleet was captured or burned in Ostia, the port of Rome, and the Appian Road was raided. In 67 the tribune, Aulus Gabinius, proposed that Pompey be vested with enormous powers throughout the empire for three years and the command of great numbers of ships and men to destroy the pirates. His bill was strongly opposed in the Senate, which only avoided massacre at the hands of a furious mob by timely dispersal. Two opposing tribunes were shouted down; when one attempted to interpose his veto, he was threatened with Octavius' fate and withdrew. Cicero was to defend Gabinius' action by pleading that 'he did not allow the voice and will of a single colleague to have more weight than those of the whole state' (Asconius, 72, C); the doctrine, which was that of Tiberius Gracchus, was one he certainly repudiated later and probably never approved at heart. In a few months Pompey swept the seas with incomparable efficiency. A new tribunician law, moved by Gaius Manilius in 66, conferred on him the command in the eastern war, which was still dragging on. Very few optimates opposed it. Pompey's power was so vast already that the new command hardly seemed to add to it materially.

There was overwhelming popular enthusiasm for the Gabinian law. It should not be ascribed mainly to pressure by the commercial classes. Of course trade suffered from the pirates' activity, but traders were not influential; Cicero lays more stress on the damage sustained by the publicans. But the chief victims were the populace. When the price of grain rose high, they starved. Pompey made it his first task to clear the sea-routes to Sardinia, Sicily and Africa, the main sources of wheat for the capital. On the very day of his appointment there was a sudden drop from a scarcity price to a low level. In fact all classes must have concurred in desiring to end depredations so injurious not only to all material interests but to Roman prestige. The Senate itself had had the wish, but had not found the means; it was convicted of incompetence, and if any justification were needed for the revival of tribunician power, it was now supplied, when tribunician initiative promoted essential action the Senate had failed to take. Gabinius' law on piracy did not stand alone; he and his colleague, Cornelius, undertook other reforms, neglected or opposed by the Senate. One perhaps deserves notice. It was the custom of the praetors, who were responsible for civil jurisdiction, to announce by edicts when taking office what remedies they would allow; by creating new forms of remedy, they were continually adjusting the law to meet new social and economic needs. But they were not required to follow their edicts in actual decisions. Thus the law was uncertain, and undue influence could affect its course. Cornelius prescribed that in future praetors must not deviate from their own edicts.

But though the tribunician legislation of 67 met real

and even urgent needs, it was natural for the optimates to resist the conferment of vast powers on Pompey. Gabinius was his associate and was later to owe the consulship of 58 to him; Pompey's ambition was as much or more the motive force behind his measure as the interest of the state. In retrospect Sallust thought that Pompey had restored tribunician rights only to facilitate his personal aggrandizement. The forces at his disposal made him potentially master of the state. The Manilian law merely confirmed the danger. Of course there would have been none, if the soldiers had been bound to the republic rather than to their general. No one in the United States had reason to apprehend that General Eisenhower could seize power when he returned victorious from Germany.

Events were to show that Pompey had no ambition to act like Sulla on his return; morally, he would have needed the kind of provocation that the Marians gave Sulla, if he was to seize absolute power. Those who knew him best probably entertained least fear of his aiming at tyranny, but his rivals had no wish to see him even pre-eminent. Crassus in particular tried to build up his own influence, to counter Pompey's. In 70 he had had the larger following in the Senate, and his readiness to grant loans, free of interest, always made him strong there. He now sought a wider popularity, with a coadjutor in Gaius Julius Caesar, a young patrician distinguished as yet only for his extravagance and debts, for his eloquence, for his flaunting his supposed descent from the gods (his family had in fact been of little note) and his undoubted kinship to Marius, and for his declared opposition to the optimates; in 64 he sought to convict as murderers men who had killed those proscribed by Sulla and in 63 he was behind the prosecution of an elderly senator, Rabirius, who had taken part in lynching Saturninus; he professed to condemn the arbitrary punishment of citizens. His popular stand combined with massive bribery to obtain for him in 63 election as Pontifex Maximus, head of the state religion.

Both Crassus and Caesar had sought to confer the citizenship on those people in north Italy, mainly beyond the Po, who had been granted only Latin rights in 89 by a law that Pompey's father had moved. That made them clients of Pompey; if they owed a higher status to Crassus and Caesar, their allegiance might shift. The attempt was foiled; Caesar ultimately enfranchised them in 49. Pompey was adding enormously to the public revenues (p. 39); Crassus and Caesar proposed to do likewise by annexing Egypt, where the title of the reigning king was uncertain; one of his predecessors had (it was said) bequeathed the realm to Rome. Here too they failed (65); in 59 Pompey, Crassus and Caesar were actually to engineer the recognition of the king in return for a huge bribe. Crassus and Caesar seem also to have instigated an agrarian bill moved by the tribune Rullus in 63. The plan was to distribute not only public land but lands that might be bought from willing sellers, largely with the new money Pompey was bringing in. Our knowledge of it derives entirely from speeches in which Cicero, who was now consul, undoubtedly misrepresents it. In his second speech on the Agrarian Law (70) he decried a saying of Rullus that 'the urban populace had too much power in the state and ought to be drained away', just as if it were 'bilge-water', a comparison which privately he found appropriate (*To Atticus* I, 19, 4). But there are other indications that the beneficiaries were to be rustics, including no doubt those who had but recently lost their lands under economic pressure and sought shelter in the city. Moreover it may have been known, or could easily be foreseen, that Pompey would require allotments for his veterans. If Rullus' bill had become law, Pompey would have returned to find a land-commission, from which he was excluded, already in control of all available sources of land, and though it would doubtless have provided for the veterans, the credit and patronage would have gone to the commissioners, probably to Crassus and Caesar above all, and not to Pompey. Cicero, who detested agrarian legislation in general and was among other things a self-constituted watchdog for Pompey, artfully disparaged the scheme, which did not interest those long domiciled in Rome. A veto was threatened and it was abandoned or defeated. But Caesar's agrarian legislation in 59 was to follow similar lines.

Crassus and Caesar also sought to place their friends in key posts; this was no more than all influential politicians attempted. Thus they backed the candidature of Gaius Antonius and Lucius Sergius Catilina for the consulship of 63. Both were disreputable figures, especially Catiline. He had made his mark as one of Sulla's most bloodthirsty agents, and if all allegations are true, had since distinguished himself by a series of crimes. But he was the scion of a decayed patrician house, had great personal charm, fascinating to Rome's gilded youth, and had pursued an orthodox political career, culminating in the most approved fashion in the misgovernment of Africa. Perhaps the support of Crassus and Caesar, whose intrigues aroused suspicion, did more than the ill qualities of Antonius and Catiline to make the nobility back the new man, Cicero, who enjoyed the support of the Equites. Despite some popular utterances and aspersions on oligarchic exclusiveness, he had never impugned the authority of the Senate and, once accepted in the ruling class, could be counted on to employ his influence and oratory in their defence. That was what he did, for instance, in successfully resisting Rullus' bill and defending Rabirius.

As early as 66 Cicero, who was of a good equestrian family, had affirmed that all senators, except a few who sought a monopoly of power, desired the Equites to be next to them in dignity or rank and to be closely bound to them in a political *entente* (*For Cluentius* 152). He always remained faithful to this ideal of unity between the orders and later broadened it to embrace the propertied class throughout Italy. His watchwords were 'the concord of the orders' and 'the consensus of Italy'. All good men in fact had an interest in preserving 'otium cum dignitate', which we may paraphrase as an ordered state in which men were valued according to their rank in a hierarchical social structure. 'Good citizens' he observed in 43 (*Philippics* XIII, 16) 'are made in the first place by nature, but fortune helps. The safety of the state is to the advantage

of all good men, but most clearly benefits men of fortune.'
He could refer privately to 'my army of the rich' (*To
Atticus* I, 19, 4), 'those whose fortunes had been augmented and accumulated by the favour of heaven' (*Against
Catiline* IV, 19). The common people he despised—'the
wretched half-starved populace, which attends mass meetings and sucks the blood of the treasury' (*To Atticus* I, 16,
11). Consequently he had no use for anything that
savoured of democracy. He objected to a secret ballot,
and conceded only with reluctance that the restoration of
tribunician power had been necessary to appease the
populace. Greek democracies had been ruined by the 'un-
restrained freedom and license of assemblies'; it was too
easy for demagogues to stir up 'artisans and shopkeepers
and all that kind of scum' (*For Flaccus* 15–18); in his view
all manual occupations were mean and sordid, unfitting
people for a share in political decisions. It was only for the
sake of stability that the people should be given the minimum of political liberty that would make them content.
In democracy men were not graded by rank and the vital
principle was ignored, which the Roman centuriate
organization displayed, that 'the greatest number should
not have the greatest power' (*Republic* I, 43; II, 39, 57).

This was vital, because the majority, being poor, might
use power to assail property rights. According to views
Cicero took over from the Greek philosopher, Panaetius,
the state existed to maintain justice, i.e. to prevent one
man harming another (unless provoked) and to ensure
that each should have the use of what he owned himself,
and all alike the use of what ought to be enjoyed in common, apparently fire, water, and good advice! (*Offices* I,
52). Men had a positive duty to make money, and though
they were urged to be beneficent, they must not go so far
as to dissipate their patrimony. It was the prime duty of
the statesman to ensure that by equity in the law and the
courts each man should keep his own and that 'while the
weaker should not be ruined on account of their lowly
status the rich should not be prevented by envy from keeping or recovering what was theirs'. Cicero illustrated these
precepts from examples in Roman history to show how

redistributions of land or cancellations of debt must always be condemned (*ibid.* II, 72–87).

In a manifesto of his political creed delivered in 56 (*For Sestius* 99 ff.) he defined the bases of 'otium cum dignitate' as preservation of the cults and auspices, the powers of magistrates and authority of the Senate, the laws and ancestral customs, the courts and jurisdiction (by which the laws were upheld), credit, the provinces and allies, the prestige of the empire, the military strength of Rome and the solvency of the treasury. All this amounted to maintaining the political and social *status quo*. The cults and auspices were important, as he avows elsewhere, because they could be manipulated to obstruct 'seditious' measures. Credit—the Latin term *fides*, which also means 'good faith' has a finer moral resonance—was essential to property rights; 'nothing is so efficacious in holding the state together' (*Offices* II, 84). And in the name of the treasury, from which the great men drew vast sums, 'largesses' of land and grain could always be opposed, even when they were not infringements of the legal or customary rights of private possessors.

The list omits one ideal to which Cicero also attached the highest value, that liberty 'which consists not in having a just master, but in having none' (*Republic* II, 43). But his concept of liberty was that of the highly placed senator, who claimed the right to form and utter his independent judgement in deliberations by which the policy of the state was decided, not that of the common man whom he would have normally excluded from a share in such decisions. It was this senatorial liberty that Augustus was to destroy. That was why he had to kill Cicero before realizing most of Cicero's other objectives.

No doubt Cicero developed his views in a more elaborate and theoretical way than most members of the upper classes would or could have done, but his theories corresponded so well with their interests and generally with their actions that we may take them as representative. They were articulated so clearly and their practical implications brought out so explicitly, precisely because they were under challenge; men seldom feel the need to state and justify their beliefs when those beliefs are universally shared. Not indeed that there was any rival political or social philosophy fully worked out. The established structure was under attack only by agitators, often or always self-interested adventurers, whose professed aim was merely to redress particular grievances, and the popular movements at Rome lacked the moral fervour as well as the intellectual basis which such a creed as Marxism may lend to modern counterparts. None the less, the threat to all that Cicero valued was grave.

Order itself was breaking down. Violence had been an occasional phenomenon before the Social war: it was now becoming endemic in the city as in the countryside. Both the tribunes Gabinius and Manilius had already resorted to it. We begin in 66 to hear of hired gangs of thugs, partly composed of gladiators and runaway slaves. Sallust and Cicero both speak of a class of professional 'dagger-men' (*sicarii*). The law forbade men to carry arms with criminal intent on pain of death, but it could hardly be enforced. The city was ungarrisoned and unpoliced. The magistrates had only a few attendants. The explanation must be conjectural; perhaps the nobility itself were afraid to entrust police-power to any one of their own number. At the end of 66 the trial of Manilius had been broken up by force; Catiline, who appeared armed in the forum, had some part in the affair. Stories circulated that he, or others, had planned then or later to massacre the Senate and seize power; they grew in the telling, and people were ready to inculpate their enemies, especially when they were ruined or dead and could not make a reply; even Crassus and Caesar suffered from these slanders.[1] But the mere fact that some found them credible indicates the prevalent insecurity.

The *collegia* played an increasing part in the disorder. Some of these were associations of craftsmen, including those which reputedly went back to the monarchy (pp. 28 f.); many more had since come into existence.

[1] See R. Seager, *Historia* 1964, 338 ff. The account of this affair by M. Cary in *Cambridge Ancient History* IX, Chapter XI, is a fantasy; in general the chapter is unreliable.

Others were composed of men who celebrated the same cults or who lived in the same neighbourhood. All were basically local. Craftsmen congregated together, and people who lived in the same district used to worship at shrines in the local crossways. These *collegia* all had elected officers, and by their agency it was easy to raise them for a demonstration or riot, just as the *menu peuple* in the French Revolution were raised through the *sections*. In 64 the Senate by decree abolished *collegia* which were 'contrary to the interest of the Republic' and forbade the celebration of the cults at crossways. Its right to act in this way was questionable, and it is rather strange that the order seems to have been effective.

Cicero tended to associate the 'egentes' (needy) with the 'perditi' (almost 'criminals'); he came near regarding poverty as a crime. It was surely a source of crime. The condition of the urban populace was wretched in the extreme. Most of them could only hope for casual employment, especially in the season of navigation, when supplies had to be unloaded and distributed. There was always private building in progress, as the city grew, but there were few great public works until the 50s, when Pompey completed a stone theatre to seat 40,000 and Caesar began to finance costly constructions. Grain was free to none and cheap only to a small minority. The poor, crammed together in a density seven or eight times that of a modern English town, lived in tenements, often sixty, seventy or more feet high, shoddily built and constantly collapsing, ill-lit, ill-ventilated, with no adequate means of cooking. (Until the second century, Pliny says, there had been no bakers; but now it was not possible for the poor to bake at home.) Water was not laid on, and there was no connection between ordinary homes and the admirable sewers; indeed the city's water supply, available to the majority at public fountains, must again have become insufficient; by building new aqueducts and repairing old, Augustus was roughly to double it. There was no fire brigade, and in the frequent conflagrations men must often have lost their scanty personal belongings, if not their lives. Nor were efficient precautions yet taken against the severe floods to which the Tiber is always liable. But the landlords did well. In 44 Cicero set aside rents he received from slum property to maintain his son as a student at Athens; he allowed him enough to pay 160 legionaries at pre-Caesarian rates. In the same year he reported that two of his shops or tenements had fallen down and that cracks were showing in others; the mice as well as the tenants had fled; but he hoped to rebuild profitably. Crassus derived much of his wealth from buying up urban property cheap when fires occurred.

The urban poor must often have been behind in paying the rent; though we only hear of arrears in rent as a serious problem after 49, this must explain their interest in a cancellation of debts in 63. At that time, according to Cicero, the burden of debt had never been greater. It affected every corner of Italy. Sullan veterans complained in a letter of autumn 63, the substance, if not the text, of which Sallust has preserved (*Catiline* 33), that 'wretched and indigent, they had mostly been deprived by the violence and cruelty of usurers of their fatherland, and all of their repute and fortunes; . . . after loss of their patrimony they were not allowed to retain the freedom of their persons'. This seems to mean that after being sold up they were compelled to work off the remainder of their debt by labouring for their creditors, in violation (they argued) of the old law by which *nexum* had been abolished (p. 57). It is curious that in 37 Varro (I, 17) implies that such a class of debt-bondsmen was extinct in Italy. Perhaps the shortage of slaves consequent on Spartacus' revolt created a temporary demand for this new kind of dependent labour; perhaps Caesar as dictator released the debt-bondsmen, or they escaped by enlistment in the inflated armies of the next generation. Cicero and other ancient writers ascribed the distress of the veterans solely to luxury and extravagance, implausible as a general explanation, though some may naturally have been improvident. In modern times it has been supposed that they were unfitted for rural life by urban antecedents or by long service with the legions; the premises are false (pp. 98 f., 108). We need look no further for the cause of their failure than the adverse economic conditions in Italy traced above. They asked for the renewal of that law of the 80s under which debts had been scaled down by three quarters. Earlier in the year a tribune had already made an abortive proposal for relief of debtors. All this was a grave danger to Cicero's sacred principle of good faith or credit.

Defeated at the polls in 64, Catiline stood again in 63; apparently without the backing of Crassus and Caesar, he turned to the discontented. He appeared in public with a motley throng of Sullan veterans and of peasants they had supplanted, now associated in common misery. In the Senate he declared that there were two bodies in the Republic, one weak with a feeble head (he meant Cicero), the other strong but lacking a head, which he would provide if it deserved his help (i.e. if it elected him). He was heavily in debt, though covered, he claimed, by his estates, and was reputed to have said that the wretched could find no sincere champion who was not wretched himself. All this portended a programme of debt-cancellation and land-distribution, which was the object of his later conspiracy. It cannot have appealed to the upper classes who controlled the electoral assembly; probably Catiline rested his hopes on intimidation. Cicero conducted the elections with a strong guard of his partisans and ostentatiously wearing a breastplate. Catiline was rejected. He had no further chance of advancing his career legally, nor perhaps of staving off bankruptcy, and he began to plan an armed coup.

His supporters included other nobles (notably a praetor, Publius Cornelius Lentulus) whose finances, like his, were embarrassed and who sought wealth and power from revolution, all sorts of criminals and adventurers, and more important, indebted and needy people throughout Rome and Italy. Sallust lays special emphasis on the urban plebs and on 'the young men who had sustained a life of want by hiring out their labour in the fields but, attracted by public and private largesses, had come to prefer idleness in the city to unrewarding toil' (*Catiline* 37). The truth is surely that these countrymen who had been unable to make a living without land favoured Catiline, because he offered them land in a new deal. While the urban plebs was not faithful to Catiline, outbreaks on his behalf are attested in Etruria (which had suffered most from Sulla's settlement) and in almost every region of Italy—Cisalpine Gaul, Picenum, Umbria, the Abruzzi, Campania, Apulia and Bruttium. The conspiracy indicated the extent and intensity of *agrarian* discontent.

There was an armed rising in Etruria in October. Cicero could as yet produce no proof of Catiline's complicity to convince his peers, but his menaces induced Catiline to leave Rome and take command. Vigorous precautions were taken. To every area of unrest senators were sent with full powers of repression, troops were levied, garrisons installed at threatened points; in Rome itself Cicero was guarded by a band of 'select young men', his clients from Reate. Mommsen despised Cicero as a word-spinner, 'valiant in opposition to sham attacks', who 'knocked down many walls of pasteboard with a loud din'; in fact he proved himself a vigilant and resolute head of state, and his prompt counter-measures explain why outside Etruria the plots or risings came to little. Naturally all the propertied citizens were at one in the crisis, and Cicero rejoiced that his ideal of the harmony of the orders had been realized.

Catiline hoped that his friends at Rome would seize control of the city; but in December Cicero at last found decisive evidence of their guilt; Lentulus and others were arrested and put to death. Most of Catiline's followers then deserted, and early in 62 the remainder were destroyed in battle, Catiline himself dying at their head. So little came of the affair that it has been said that it would make hardly any difference to our understanding of subsequent events, if we knew nothing of it. That is a superficial view. Cicero, it is true, had a strong motive to magnify his achievement and to pose as the saviour of the state. But Sallust, not one of his admirers, regarded it as the most signal proof of Rome's moral degeneration that 'there were citizens firmly resolved to ruin themselves and the state, . . . such was the force of the disease whose infection had invaded the minds of *most* citizens' (*Catiline* 36). This alienation from the Republic may be ascribed rather to economic and social than to moral causes, and it was most apparent in the rural areas, where the soldiers were recruited.

The urban plebs had been detached from the conspirators by Cicero's allegation that they planned to burn the city down; even the humblest would then lose the place where they sat and worked and earned their daily bread and the couch on which they slept (*Against Catiline* IV, 17). By the end of the year there was a revulsion of feeling. Cicero had executed Lentulus and his accomplices without trial on the authority of a decree of the Senate, opposed by Caesar and moved by a junior senator, Marcus Porcius Cato, whose ability and steely resolution henceforth combined with his high birth and character to make him the most influential leader of the optimates. It was a plain breach of Gaius Gracchus' law (p. 89), and if nobles like Lentulus could be put to death untried, the common man had even less assurance of personal protection. An agitation against Cicero began before he laid down office. Never again did he enjoy the popularity he had claimed before. He confessed to Atticus in 49 that 'wicked' citizens somehow found it popular to attack him.

To maintain order and its authority a concession had to be made. Pompey's conquests had enormously increased the treasury's resources, and in 62 Cato, who was tribune, himself extended the cheap grain distributions, probably to all free inhabitants of Rome.

At the end of that year Pompey returned from the east. By disbanding his army at once he showed that he had no unconstitutional aims; indeed he made overtures to the nobility for their friendship. But he had affronted too many of them, and they persistently obstructed his demands that the Senate should ratify without question all the many decisions he had made on the future government of the east and that allotments of land should be given to his veterans. Thus they drove him into alliance with Caesar, who could not be kept out of the consulship of 59. Caesar had advocated the Gabinian law, and despite his association with Crassus, had never broken with Pompey. He was now able to bring Crassus into a coalition, which we call the first triumvirate. Caesar was ready to place the consular authority and his demagogic arts at the disposal of Pompey in return for a great province, which the Senate had denied him (p. 117).

Filibustering in the Senate soon led Caesar to submit an agrarian bill direct to the Assembly. Pompey made it clear that violent obstruction would be met by force, and it was carried by the strong arms of his veterans. Opposing tribunes were simply driven from the forum. Caesar's colleague, Marcus Calpurnius Bibulus, retired for the rest of the year to his house and gave out that he was watching the sky for omens; he argued that, as these might be unfavourable, no business could legally be transacted; this unexampled abuse of the religious law put Caesar technically in the wrong, and his adversaries proclaimed their intention of bringing him to trial, as soon as he had become a private citizen. For the time being the triumvirs could act more or less as they pleased, so long as they were united. The Senate was virtually reduced to the role of an opposition. Pompey's eastern settlement was ratified. The Asian publicans' demand for a remission of part of the sum they had contracted to pay the treasury was granted. The Senate's failure to concede the demand had temporarily shattered the concord of the orders, but even if the rift had not occurred, the course of events in 59 would not have been materially different; the Equites did not control the political balance, nor were they united among themselves; in the summer there were equestrian demonstrations against the triumvirs, for which the country gentry were doubtless responsible. The triumvirs' dominance rested on force, at first on the backing of Pompey's veterans, later on the proximity of the great army Caesar secured in Gaul.

Caesar's agrarian legislation (there were two laws) provided that the veterans and 20,000 of the poor, who had three or more children, should receive allotments from a commission, partly from public domain, partly from lands the commission might buy with the new revenues from willing sellers at values fixed in the census returns. Even the rich Campanian land, which had been leased by the state since 211 and which the Gracchi had not touched, was to be available, but it is unlikely that small farmers there lost the land they had leased; even the middling landholders who formed the town council of Capua were not disturbed, and Cicero was probably right in estimating that there was land here only for 5,000 settlers; this amount was surrendered by Roman capitalists. The veterans alone can hardly have numbered under 25,000, and if we add 20,000 other proletarians, the scheme may have provided for some 50,000 allotments and have done more to revive the peasantry than Sulla had achieved, since no existing smallholders were now to be expropriated. Though we know hardly anything of the commission's activity, they must at least have satisfied the veterans; on this point silence is proof.

In 58, through not in all the succeeding years, friends of the triumvirs were consuls; more important, they had a useful collaborator in Publius Clodius as tribune. He was a patrician by birth, but in 59 Caesar as chief pontiff had sanctioned his adoption into a plebeian family, which qualified him for the tribunate. This did not make him a tool of the triumvirs; no member of his proud family was ever at anyone's beck and call, and he was bent on building up his own influence, but he assisted the triumvirs by removing from the scene two men who could have given them trouble. One was Cato; Clodius promoted a law to annex Cyprus under which Cato was appointed to organize the new province. He did not venture to refuse, and hence could hardly now impugn the validity of Caesar's acts in 59; if they were null, so was Clodius' adoption, and Clodius had no right to be tribune or to propose legislation. Nor could he assail the popular principle that the people might grant extraordinary commands like his own. Cicero was more harshly treated; Clodius had a personal grudge against him and drove him into exile.

Clodius first promulgated a bill which outlawed any one who had put to death an unconvicted citizen. This was plainly aimed at Cicero, who implored the protection of Senate and Equites, the consuls and the triumvirs. But the consuls had been bribed by Clodius with the promise of rich provincial commands, and Pompey and Caesar, subordinating old ties of friendship to present interests, maintained an overt neutrality that abandoned Cicero to his enemy. Nearly all the other tribunes were against Clodius, but he was master of the streets, and given the attitude of the consuls and of Caesar, who was still outside Rome, recruiting troops, he could not be overawed by higher authority or superior force. Cicero fled; he was then formally banished and his property confiscated. Symbolically, Clodius dedicated the site of his town house to the spirit of Liberty which Cicero had defied by violating the rights of citizens.

This measure was popular in itself, but Clodius had already fortified his dominance in the city by other laws. One, which forbade for the future the abuse of religious obstructions that Bibulus had practised, only removed an impediment to popular sovereignty. More important, he made the corn doles free, thus overtrumping Cato's law (p. 132), and legalized without restriction that right of association which the Senate's abolition of certain *collegia* in 64 infringed (p. 128). He thus gained a following in the city, which made him, unlike earlier popular tribunes, a force in politics even when he was out of office.

The abolition of the charge for public grain rations was followed by a vast increase in the number of recipients. By about 46 it had risen to 320,000 males over ten. No doubt the prospect of free grain encouraged further immigration from the country, but free grain alone did not sustain life, and the chances of employment, though enhanced by the new public building programmes, were limited. As dictator, Caesar was to cut the number to 150,000, and though he arranged for perhaps 70,000 of the urban plebs to settle overseas, we still have a gap of about 100,000; what sort of people did he exclude? Probably some who were not entitled to be on the list at all and whom Pompey tried to remove in 55. Romans often manumitted slaves without going through the formal legal process, which attracted a tax; their freedom was precarious and rested on the readiness of the praetor to uphold it, if their old masters sought to reduce them to servitude once more; it was left to Augustus, or Tiberius, to regularize their status, and to guarantee them freedom with certain disabilities. They were not citizens, but conceivably were illegally registered for the citizen doles. Further, even when the legal forms were observed, the master could put the freedman under a legal obligation to work for him in return for his keep or sufficient wages for his maintenance. As maintenance was now in part provided by the state, it must often have been the cheapest course for masters to free slaves on these terms. I conjecture that Caesar, disapproving their action, excluded freedmen who had been manumitted from a certain date. But his rules were not observed on his death; in summer 44 there were again 250,000 recipients of the dole, and by 5 BC 320,000; three years later Augustus restricted entitlement to 200,000, on what principle we do not know.

These figures are the only evidence for the size of the urban population in this epoch. We do not know how many free females or boys under ten there were, nor how many remained slaves. But most of the inhabitants of Rome were apparently of servile origin, and masters did not require nearly as many women as men; there was little employment for them except in textile work, and as slaves could be bought cheap when fully grown and immediately profitable, women were not much needed to bear slave children. Moreover such slave children as there were could be reared at less cost in the country. As for the freeborn poor, they found it hard to raise children; exposure of babies was presumably common, and probably affected girls more than boys. Thus the proportion of females and boys under ten should have been low. The number of slaves was probably reduced by large-scale manumissions in the 50s. I do not think that we need set the total population higher than 750,000. Certainly less than half the free inhabitants received the doles. At five *modii* a month they were ample for single persons, insufficient for families. The market price of grain was therefore still important to the poor.

Once the *collegia* had been legalized, Clodius set about organizing them on a para-military basis, almost in battalions and companies, and distributing arms. Cicero would have it that they were composed of slaves, especially runaways, criminals ('assassins from the jail'), and at best hirelings. This may be doubted. He himself lets out that it was a rhetorical trick to call people who went to political meetings 'exiles, slaves, madmen', and he was capable of describing freedmen as slaves. Contemporaries said of mobs in eighteenth- and nineteenth-century England and France that they consisted of desperadoes, ragamuffins, convicts; but whenever records can be found, they generally reveal craftsmen, shopkeepers and respectable labourers. The Catilinarians had appealed to 'the *artisans* and slaves', and Cicero mentions *shopkeepers* among Clodius' followers; he notes too that seditious tribunes, when they wished to raise a mob, had the shops closed. Now in a famine of 41 the people spontaneously closed their shops; earlier riots too were probably not so much fomented by agitators as provoked by distress. No doubt Clodius owed his hold over the mob primarily to the gratitude he had earned; but perhaps even he had to play on continuing grievances, to bring shopkeepers from their counters and craftsmen from their benches.

While still tribune, Clodius quarrelled with Pompey, who was terrified into keeping to his house for months. In 57 Pompey determined to have Cicero recalled. As a preliminary, an optimate tribune, Titus Annius Milo, had to muster hired bands, including gladiators, to contest the streets with Clodius' supporters. (It is noteworthy that the nobility were still able to win most elections, even for the tribunate.) Finally, Pompey organized the respectable people throughout Italy to come to Rome with their retainers and vote Cicero's recall in the centuries which they could dominate. He had an enthusiastic reception, by his own account even from the 'lowest plebs'; if that was true, it was the crowd emotion of the moment, the volatility he himself loved to censure.

At the time of his banishment there had been a food shortage; Cicero observed that men pulling his house down were not going to satisfy their appetite on tiles and cement; this implies that they were hungry. It was one thing to enact that men were to have grain free, another to procure it. Clodius' law probably increased demand, without increasing the supply. The concourse for Cicero's recall must have aggravated scarcity. In July and September 57 there were food riots. Prices oscillated, and the mob turned out when they were high, not just when Clodius found it convenient. It became necessary to entrust Pompey with an extraordinary commission for five years to procure grain. The price sank as if by magic, but Pompey was no magician, and the organization of supplies took time. In February, April and August 56 we hear again of high prices, infertility of the fields, poor harvests. Hunger was the background of the constant violence in the 50s, perhaps more often than we know. On one occasion of uproar Clodius accused Pompey himself of starving the people.

If this were a political history, it would be indispensable to recount and analyse the complex manœuvres of the triumvirs, Clodius and the leading optimates in the following years. That is not our subject, and there is no space. In 56 the triumvirs, who had been drifting apart, renewed their compact. Caesar was to retain his great province until 50 or (on the orthodox view) until 49. Pompey and Crassus, in return, became consuls in 55, and while Crassus went out to fight the Parthians (by whom he was killed), Pompey was allotted the government of Spain, which he conducted through legates or deputies, remaining just outside Rome to see that the will of the triumvirs was not flouted; the arrangement anticipated those by which Augustus administered provinces. But he lacked authority to maintain order in the city, where violence and bloodshed became the rule. In 57 the tribune, Sestius, had been left for dead on the streets. In November 56 Cicero was suddenly attacked by Clodius' gangs with shouts, stones, clubs, swords, and only saved by his escort. Next day Clodius tried to burn down Milo's house in broad daylight and was nearly killed in a counter-attack. Pompey and Crassus could obtain election only by violence. In 54 the disorder was such that no consuls could be elected for the following year; it had run half its course before any were returned. Early in 52 there were again no magistrates except tribunes in office. Then Clodius was murdered by Milo near the city. In fury the mob burned his body along with the Senate house and the adjacent Porcian basilica in a great funeral pyre. They killed any one they met wearing fine clothes or gold rings.[1] The houses of many eminent men were threatened. Class hatred is patent. At last the optimates, who had sometimes fomented the anarchy to embarrass Pompey, had to turn to him for aid. He was made sole consul, and with the help of troops restored order.

Reconciled to Pompey, the optimates had not forgiven Caesar and still designed to bring him to book for his offences in 59. Pompey had become jealous of his former ally and showed no disposition to guarantee his safety from prosecution by conceding him the right to stand for a second consulship in absence and enter upon it immediately after his command had terminated. The conqueror of Gaul and darling of the mob would then have been pre-eminent in the state, displacing Pompey. The Senate wished to supersede him at the earliest possible date: tribunes, friendly to Caesar, vetoed its decrees. In January 49, relying on two legions Pompey already had in Italy and on his assumed ability quickly to raise more, if needed, the Senate passed 'the last decree' (p. 90) and threatened the personal safety of the Caesarian tribunes, if they persisted with their veto. They fled to Caesar, and he marched into Italy. Pompey's forces were inadequate; the towns opened their gates to the invader; new recruits dispersed, or enlisted under Caesar. Pompey withdrew across the Adriatic with such troops as he could keep together. In successive campaigns (49 and 48) Caesar destroyed his armies, in Spain, then in the East; Pompey was killed as a refugee in Egypt. The survivors of his party were able to organize new resistance, first in Africa, which

[1] Only senators and Equites were entitled to wear gold rings.

Caesar conquered in 46 (Cato died here by his own hand), then again in Spain, where they were crushed in 45. But Caesar had been master of Rome and Italy since 49, and of most of the empire since 48; he ruled autocratically as dictator, and the later wars only limited the time he had to take other measures which the crisis, or more permanent defects in the political and economic structure, suggested to his own mind.

In 49 the Pompeians claimed to be fighting for the authority of the Senate, Caesar for the sanctity of tribunes and liberty of the people, oppressed by a small faction which had terrorized the Senate itself into passing its fatal decrees. (It was perfectly true that the majority of the Senate would have accepted a peaceful compromise but was overawed by its leading figures.) Although each party laid its constitutional case before citizens and soldiers, it is unlikely that many were influenced by this propaganda. Caesar did not conceal that he was also contending for his 'dignity', the rank he had earned by his offices and achievements. Dignity, he said, was preferable for him to life; he did not add that it was preferable to the lives of thousands of fellow-citizens, who were to perish in the war. His enemies alleged that he aimed at *regnum*, despotism. His willingness to settle for terms, under which he would not have had control but merely the first place in the Republic, shows that this was not his original design; but when war and victory thrust absolute power upon him, he gladly took it; the Republic, he allegedly said, was an insubstantial phantom, and Sulla by his abdication had proved that he did not know the ABC of politics. But were his opponents less disinterested? At times even Cicero thought that Pompey as well as Caesar sought to be 'king'. And whereas Caesar was persistent in pardoning his adversaries, they looked forward to proscribing the Caesarians and sharing out the spoils.

At first it was widely expected that Caesar would himself proscribe his enemies, redistribute land and cancel debts. The rich, Equites as well as senators, inclined to Pompey. But these fears were soon allayed. In 49 Caesar displayed as much respect for legal correctness and pro-

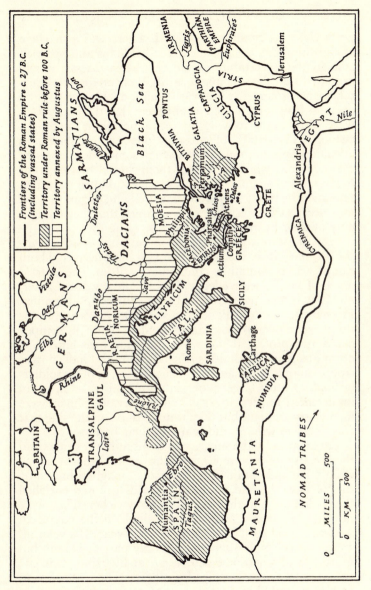

4. Roman Empire in 27 B.C.

perty rights as conditions allowed. There was a shortage of cash in circulation, as men recalled loans and hoarded coin in the uncertainty of the crisis, but Caesar merely provided that debtors might satisfy their creditors by surrendering property at pre-war valuations. He had rapidly overrun Italy, and it became apparent that the Pompeians were only likely to win by reconquering it in Sulla's fashion. Their talk of proscriptions and confiscations alienated opinion, especially as they sometimes suggested that everyone who was not for them should be treated as having been against them. Most men of property had remained in Italy; they were alarmed, and began to hope for Caesar's triumph. Cicero complained that they thought only of their farms and moneybags.

Men often took sides because of personal ties of friendship or allegiance. But one man might have friends in both camps, and communities conflicting loyalties. The Italians north of the Po were clients of both Pompey and Caesar, but Caesar was in control, and they enlisted in his armies. Picenum was an old Pompeian stronghold, yet the towns there went over to Caesar without a blow; if Pompey could not protect them, what did they owe him? The optimate, Lucius Domitius Ahenobarbus, did indeed raise troops among his tenantry and clients, but to other soldiers he had to offer large allotments from his estates, as an inducement to their loyalty. Without avail; soldiers were mercenary enough, but they wanted to be on the side that was likely to win. So did many of their betters.

Caesar won by the superiority of his military genius and the loyalty of his veteran Gallic army, under 40,000 strong. He had obtained it by personal magnetism and by the 'services' he had rendered them. Booty had enriched them already, and they hoped to grow richer. They were not disappointed. Caesar roughly doubled the pay of all soldiers, bringing it up to 225 *denarii* a year. His veterans were to receive on discharge not only parcels of land but gratuities of 5,000 or 6,000 *denarii* at his triumph in 46, with proportionately more for officers. Their attachment to him outlasted his life; they were passionate for revenge on his assassins. Between 49 and 44 he enlisted probably some 200,000 other soldiers, whom he had recruited himself or taken over from the Pompeians. They felt no such devotion to him. Most of them were conscripts. They had had no wish to serve, but once in the army, they sought to make the best of it; in the wars after Caesar's death they would generally fight for the highest bidder, no less for his assassins than for his heir or friends.

Some of the Pompeians had certainly believed that the survival of the Republic rested on their success; Brutus and Cassius of course took the same view in 44–42, and again appealed to Republican sentiment. Liberty, as they understood it, was at stake, but it was the liberty of a few, and could be fairly represented as oligarchic domination; it made little impact on the masses, and even the respectable classes in general desired security above everything else. The wars were decided, not by the support that principles attracted, but by sheer force, a preponderance in which was secured partly by personal ties, still more by the offers of rewards which the rivals held out to the soldiers, or rather by the expectation that they could make good their promises. In the struggles the old political order was overturned; it commanded no loyalty for its own sake, and deserved none.

On his side Caesar had professed allegiance to popular principles. Having gained power, he flouted them, as Cinna had done. He took to himself the nomination of many of the magistrates and deprived the people of electoral rights. He had invaded Italy, he said, to defend the tribunes. In 44, when tribunes displeased him, he deposed them. He was a monarch, but he could not found a monarchy. Elderly himself, he had no son, no close kinsman apparently old enough to succeed—it could not be foreseen that his grand-nephew and heir, the future emperor Augustus, was sufficiently mature at the age of nineteen—and no suitable friend to whom he could hand over power. All he could do, acting with restless energy in the intervals of campaigns, was to promote useful reforms (which cannot be fully listed here), of which some evinced his old popular sympathies.

Until 46 Africa was in Pompeian hands, and Rome was

cut off from one of her chief corn suppliers. This must have raised the price of grain and occasioned much distress. When the poor had to pay more for bread, they had less in their pockets for other commitments such as rent. In 48 and 47 there were bloody riots in the city, when demands were made that rents and other debts should be remitted. A year's remission of rents at Rome had to be granted in 48, and in my view Caesar himself on his return renewed it in 47 with an upper limit of 500 *denarii*; he also relieved debtors by letting them deduct interest paid from the capital owed, apparently up to 25%. He may also have introduced a milder form of bankruptcy for debtors who had substantial property, and conceivably released from imprisonment or debt-bondage (p. 129) those who swore that they had no means to pay. If the last conjecture is right, his measure later fell into abeyance; that is possible, as we know that some law he passed relating to debt was no longer enforced in AD 33. All this was beyond Cicero's understanding. 'Are men', he wrote after Caesar's death, 'to live for nothing on the property of others? When I have bought or built a house and keep it up at my cost, are you to have the enjoyment of it without my consent? . . . What is to be said for cancellation of debts but this—you buy a farm with my cash, you have the farm, and I don't get the cash?' It was sheer robbery, and destroyed the basis of society. No marvel indeed that Caesar should have favoured such courses at a time when he was (so Cicero liked to say) an accomplice of Catiline, and encumbered with debt; but now that he was a rich man, how could it be explained? It must be due to a love of wickedness for its own sake! (*Offices* II, 84 f.).

We have seen that Caesar more than halved the number of corn-recipients. But there were grandiose building projects, some completed later, to give employment, and not only in Rome; he designed the draining of the Pontine marshes, which it was left to Mussolini to effect. Moreover 80,000 of the poor were to be found lands abroad. The total may include some of the veterans who were settled in the provinces, and perhaps others of rural origin; most were from the city. The colonists did not all go to vacant lands; it was necessary to expropriate provincials, who suffered (as usual) in the interest of the master people. The veterans, probably reduced to 20,000, were indeed mainly given allotments in Italy itself, but here Caesar sought to avoid dispossessing existing holders, except for a few who had taken possession of land in Sulla's time without title. Unlike Sulla, he consistently tried to bind up the wounds of the nation, not to open them anew.

Yet he was killed on 15 March 44, by men whom he had pardoned or who had fought for him, but who declined to be subject to a master, however beneficent. They hoped that by removing the monarch they would restore the Republic, and the power of their own class, which they doubtless sincerely identified with the public welfare. Like Caesar, they were resolved to be merciful; they did not touch his principal adherents, Marcus Aemilius Lepidus and Marcus Antonius (then consul). This was a fatal error. Cicero regretted that they had not 'invited him to the banquet; then there would have been no left-overs' (*To his friends* XII, 4, 1).

A series of adroit manœuvres soon made Antony almost master of the state. His success would have been complete if he had had the united support of all Caesar's former partisans. But some, including Caesar's veterans, resented his efforts to push on one side the young Gaius Octavius, Caesar's heir, who took Caesar's name and whom we conventionally call Octavian. For a time there was an unnatural coalition between the Senate led by Cicero (it was his heroic hour) and Octavian, which brought about Antony's defeat in north Italy and the dissolution of most of his army (43). Antony found new backing in Lepidus and the armies of the western provinces; and he now saw the necessity of a deal with Octavian. For his part Octavian desired revenge on his adoptive father's assassins, who had seized command of great armies in the East, and he had discovered, or rather confirmed, that the Senate's plan was to use him and discard him. The three dynasts joined forces, entered Rome, and proscribed their opponents. Their conception was that of Cicero, who had told Brutus that civil wars would never cease if a spurious clemency were shown to enemies; Cicero was now one of their victims. They assumed jointly autocratic powers as 'triumvirs for the constitution of the state'. In 42 they destroyed the armies of Brutus and Cassius at Philippi; the 'Liberators' perished by their own hands. Henceforth, as Tacitus wrote, there were no more Republican armies; and it only remained for the conquerors to divide and quarrel over the spoils. The question was indeed not simply who was to be master. It was conceivable that none would emerge finally victorious and that civil struggles would cease only with the disruption of the empire. In these years Horace could envisage the day when Parthian horse might clatter down the Roman streets. The Republic was ended; could any man create a new, durable system in which Rome would survive?

Octavian gave the answer. It would take too long to tell here how, in the virtual partition of the empire effected in 42 and ratified in 40, Italy, the reservoir of legionaries, came in practice under his control, while Antony undertook to settle the East and revenge Crassus' defeat by the Parthians, an enterprise which ended only in a new disaster (36), how in the meantime Octavian eliminated first Sextus, son of the great Pompey, who from a base in Sicily had established dominance of the sea, and then Lepidus (36), how he and Antony were thus left rivals face to face, how he was able to convict or misrepresent Antony as a renegade to Italian traditions, who had abandoned the interests of Rome to his 'paramour', Cleopatra, the queen of Egypt, and to organize Italian opinion in his favour, binding all the citizens by an oath of personal allegiance to himself (32), how with overwhelming superiority of force he defeated Antony at Actium (31), and how on the suicide of Antony and Cleopatra he re-united the empire under his sole sway and annexed Egypt (30).

Peace was restored, the veterans settled, lavish distributions made to the plebs, and a great building programme put in train, with most of all these costs borne by Octavian from his enormous private wealth, augmented from the spoils of Egypt. He could claim with some justice to rule with the consent of all, but he could not rule alone. He needed the co-operation of the upper class; he recognized that they had a sentimental attachment to the old Republic, and at last in 27 he affected to restore it and to become no more than the first citizen (*princeps*). But he kept for himself the most important provinces and the greatest armies, and in the remaining forty years of his long life, in which men gradually became habituated to the new system, his control tended to become tighter in every branch of government. From 23 he began to count almost as regnal years the annual tenure of the tribunician power, which had been conferred on him for life. He held it, says Tacitus (*Annals* I, 2), 'for the protection of the common people'; certainly the title was a concession to old popular traditions; we shall see later how faithfully he continued them. Command of the troops was more vital, but not the sole basis of his power. He himself claimed supremacy in *auctoritas* (p. 46), influence which was grounded above all on his continuing success in maintaining order at home and prestige abroad, and thereby securing almost universal consent. It was symbolized in his new name, Augustus, which means 'revered' and assimilated him to the gods and to Romulus, who had founded Rome 'augusto augurio', with an omen that foretold how Rome was to become, what its new ruler had apparently made it, mistress of the world.

7

Epilogue

Acriora ex eo vincula (Tacitus)

AUGUSTUS in Tacitus' view won over the soldiers with
gifts, the people with grain, and all with the delight of
order (*otium*).

Soldiers now regularly received lands or cash on discharge. Augustus claimed that he thus paid off 300,000
who had sworn obedience to him; the total should not
include about 25,000 of Antony's veterans discharged in
41–40. I reckon that at that time some 50,000 Italians
received allotments in Italy; 15,000 more were settled in
Italy or Sicily in 36. After Actium some 85,000 were
provided with lands; they included provincials and many
were placed in overseas colonies. Provincial recruitment
and settlement abroad continued thereafter, and we cannot be sure how many of the veterans discharged between
30 and AD 14, possibly 175,000, were Italians or were
settled in Italy.

The treatment of the soldiers became less favourable as
Augustus was more and more firmly ensconced in power
and was better able to restore discipline. Most of the men
discharged in 41–40 and 36 had served only about six
years; by 13 BC he fixed a term of sixteen, and in practice
men were retained with the standards for twenty, twenty-
five or longer. The triumvirs promised their troops at
Philippi, 5,000 *denarii* in addition to land; in 29 Octavian
actually paid a donative of 250 to the veterans he had
settled in military colonies; but from 13 grants of money
were an alternative to land. Henceforth the veteran was
entitled to 3,000 *denarii*. This was not affluence, but it
was over thirteen times his annual pay, already raised by
Caesar; and the Republican veteran had had no entitlement at all. It was costly, and Augustus, who had hitherto

148

EPILOGUE

paid the veterans off from his vast private resources, ultimately found it necessary (in AD 6) to provide that the soldiers' bounties should be financed from the proceeds of the tax on sales by auction in Italy and from newly imposed death-duties on the richer citizens. The imposition was accepted by the Senate under protest; had the ruling class been prepared to bear this burden in the Republic, they might conceivably have cemented the loyalty of the troops to the old régime. That loyalty was now due to the Emperor. It was to him that the soldiers were bound by the religious tie of oaths, and it was he who appointed their actual commanders; if he chose them prudently, they would be reliable men. Moreover the centurions, who had been the natural leaders of the soldiers in the mutinies and desertions common in the civil wars, were now far more handsomely remunerated and could generally be trusted to repress sedition. Military indiscipline was again to throw the empire into fearful confusion in the third century, but apart from two grave interruptions in AD 68–70 and 193–7, the Augustan system succeeded in subordinating the army to the civil power for two centuries.

The Republican legionaries had shown no loyalty to a government that evinced no care for their interests nor for the rural plebs from whom they were drawn. Augustus and his successors made adequate provision for the soldiers, but were pretty indifferent to the fate of the rural plebs. The settlement of veterans in 41–40 resembled that effected by Sulla. Like Sulla the triumvirs had confiscated great estates from their enemies, but these were sold to finance the Philippi campaign or to enrich themselves and their chief partisans, and they too were bent on concentrating the veterans in colonies as bastions of their own dominance; they designated lands and houses of sixteen of the most opulent Italian cities for their benefit. Small men, like Meliboeus in Virgil's first eclogue, had to give up their cottages roofed with turf; even the veterans complained when the victims happened to be their own or their fallen comrades' parents and children. There was no compensation and immense confusion and suffering.

149

After Actium Augustus could pay from his own pocket for the lands he took in Italy, but partisans of Antony were still expelled and settled overseas. And then as later, many of the veterans received allotments in provincial colonies, often at the expense of the natives. The net result of these operations may not have added substantially to the number of small owners in Italy.

After Tiberius (AD 14–37) conscription was seldom applied in Italy; by the second century there were few Italians in the legions. This seems to have disturbed the government. Nerva (AD 96–8) promoted a new agrarian scheme on a small scale, and soon afterwards we find that the state made funds available to assist the poor throughout Italy in maintaining children, apparently in the hope that they would eventually enlist; the hope proved vain, and we cannot tell how much this 'alimentary' scheme contributed to alleviating distress. In general, just because the government could now rely on provincial recruitment, it did not need to feel that concern for keeping up Italian manpower which had been perhaps the chief motive for Tiberius Gracchus' agrarian law. Nor could there be any future Gracchus. From the first the new régime had no room for seditious tribunes. The complaints of the poor were untold or unheard, and their misery can only be glimpsed or surmised from the one-sided record of history.

It would be wrong to suppose that small farmers had ever been eliminated in Italy. If conscription had accelerated their ruin, the various allotment schemes since 133 had at least temporarily retarded the process. Writing in the 30s, Varro noted that many poor men tilled their own fields with the help of their families. But there are signs that the concentration of property in large estates continued. Moreover the rich still preferred to rely on the labour of slave gangs. True, they also leased farms to free tenants. This was not a new development, and it may be an accident of the surviving evidence that we now hear more of it. The tenants themselves might use slave labour, often supplied by the owners along with other costly equipment under the terms of the lease. Some were wretchedly poor, in constant arrears with the rent, for

which the owners could distrain on their personal belongings. The burden of debt remained heavy. Writing about
AD 60, Columella (I, 3, 12) alludes to the immense tracts
which the great proprietors cultivated 'by means of the
bondage of citizens and by slave-gangs'; it looks as if
debtors were again being compelled to work for their
creditors, as in 63 (p. 129). Lawyers in the second century
declared that tenants were unquestionably free to leave
their farms; this suggests that attempts were being made
to detain them. Probably population was declining;
owners faced with a scarcity of labour would resort to
coercion, relying on the sanctions of the law of debt or
their political influence. In a free society the working
class could have bettered their condition, if the demand
for labour exceeded the supply, but in the Roman empire
freedom was increasingly eroded, and government was in
the hands of the upper class. By the fourth century taxation was extended to land in Italy, and as revenue would
fall off, if the fields were deserted, the government bound
rural workers, free as well as slave, to the soil; they and
their children after them had to cultivate the land where
they were born. This suited the landowner too, in so far
as it stopped his free workers taking themselves off to a
higher bidder.

Thus the rural poor in Italy, whose strong arms had
brought the Republic down, gained nothing, at least in
the long run, from the revolution. They had helped to set
up a strong régime, which no longer depended on their
support and could view their needs with indifference. Nor
is it easy to see what could have been done for them. The
various allotment schemes of the Republic had had no
lasting effect. The discontinuance of conscription did not
prove a sufficient remedy. The appetite of the rich for
land remained voracious, and bad seasons or improvidence
still placed the poor at their mercy. Slave labour continued to compete with free labour. Although war and
piracy no longer yielded so abundant a supply of cheap
slaves, there may have been no significant decline in the
use of slaves. To judge from the juristic writings of the
second and early third centuries, slaves were still dominant

in Italian trade, industry and agriculture. Perhaps breeding of slaves was now practised on a large scale; perhaps the illegal sale of free men and their children into servitude was far more common than is generally conceded. The impoverishment of free men was surely at all times correlated with extensive employment of slaves.

It was the urban plebs that Augustus won over with grain. He entertained the idea of abolishing the doles but did not venture on it, though ultimately he cut down the number of recipients (p. 136). The price of grain on the free market thus remained important, and a more efficient system for procuring overseas supplies doubtless kept it relatively low. Augustus' successors spent vast sums in fostering the corn trade and improving Rome's harbour facilities. The emperors also augmented the supply of water and took better precautions against fires and floods. Most of them were great builders in other ways; the city was adorned with temples, theatres, palaces and so forth. All this created employment for casual labour. Vespasian rejected a labour-saving device; if he were to adopt it, he asked, how could he feed his poor commons? There were also splendid shows to amuse the proletariate and their betters. Everyone recalls Juvenal's gibe that the plebs now craved for nothing but bread and circuses. It was expedient to satisfy their craving. Though the city was now better policed—counting the firemen, brigaded in semi-military units, there were after Tiberius some 20,000 soldiers in the city available to keep order—a riot was a serious matter. Octavian in 39 and Claudius later were almost lynched by hungry mobs. In AD 238 the soldiery could only get the better of the people by setting fire to the balconies of the houses; as a result much of the city was devastated. To preserve their persons from insult, if not assault, the emperors had to give the urban plebs a privileged position; provincial taxpayers footed the bill. The plebs had played a subsidiary role in the Revolution, important only at moments, for instance when they drove Cinna out of the city and set in train the series of events that led to Sulla's dictatorship, when they carried the Gabinian law by violence and thus gave Pompey his great command which proved fateful for the Republic, and when their continual turbulence in the 50s finally promoted the accord between Pompey and the optimates from which the civil war of 49 issued. But in the outcome they gained immeasurably more than the rural poor.

All, it might seem, benefited from the restoration of peace and order. 'With Caesar holding the lands,' wrote Horace (*Odes* III, 14), 'I shall not fear commotions nor death by violence.' This was the constant theme of Augustan propaganda. And it is hard to exaggerate the tumult and terror of the preceding years. Appian has a graphic account of conditions in 41, when Octavian was trying to settle the soldiers (*Civil Wars* V, 17 f.). They were completely out of hand as a result of the civil wars in which generals had become dependent on their loyalty, and pillaged as they pleased. The fields were denuded of labourers, and farmers, who feared to be dispossessed by the veterans, were reluctant to sow what others might reap. Sextus Pompey commanded the seas and virtually cut off maritime imports. Famine was endemic until his overthrow in 36. In 41 the people at Rome 'shut their shops and drove the magistrates from their seats, seeing that there was no need of crafts or magistrates in a city oppressed by want and looting'. A minor civil war occurred between the partisans of Antony and Octavian; conscription and devastations again afflicted Italy. By 40 the soldiers themselves were weary of war and forced the triumvirs to compose their quarrels. It was not till 36 that Octavian could begin to put down the brigandage and kidnapping which had long been an evil (p. 117). The fear that Italy would once more become a theatre of military operations must have contributed to enlisting public opinion on Octavian's side in 32; like the Pompeians in 49, Antony could win only by reconquering the land. Further proscriptions and confiscations might follow, and the rich had most to lose. *Otium*, peace and order under a strong government, had been one of Cicero's chief objectives, and Augustus made it a reality.

Freedom in the optimate sense was indeed lost, but

most of the old nobility who best understood it and prized it most highly perished in the wars and proscriptions; their few survivors were ready to pay the price for security, while the 'new men' from the towns of Italy, who largely supplanted the old nobility, attained higher status and greater influence than they could have expected before, not only in the Senate but in the equestrian order, which increasingly supplied the emperors with executive agents and advisers. Indeed, in the course of time access to positions of power and profit in the state was more and more widely opened to provincials as well as Italians of the upper classes.

The emperors were autocrats and many degenerated into tyrants. There was constant tension between them and the higher orders of society. The Senate, in particular, preserved an *esprit de corps* which fostered mutual distrust between its members, whatever their origins, and those emperors who frowned on the expression of independent views and even the barest hint of criticism, or who disregarded the pretence that they were only the first of citizens, hankered after the trappings of royal or even quasi-divine status, and destroyed the amenity of their personal relations with men of high rank. Some, like Domitian (AD 81–96), were made cruel by fear and rapacious by lack of money to satisfy their extravagance. The lives and fortunes of individuals were at their mercy, and reigns of terror were ended only by revolt or assassination. But all thought of reviving the Republic soon vanished. The crimes and caprices of particular emperors provoked silent resentment and occasional conspiracies, but what men desired was the removal of the ruler, not the destruction of the régime.

The régime was safe because it answered to the needs and interests of the higher orders. No single man could govern the empire unaided, and every emperor was bound to look primarily to those orders for his advisers and officials; they had almost a monopoly of the education and experience required. (To a limited extent emperors could also find assistants in their own highly trained slaves and freedmen.) The emperors might persecute individual senators or Equites, but it did not even occur to any of them (not one was a man of original views) to assail the vital interests of the whole upper class, and if they had tried, they could not have survived. It is characteristic that when Pius (AD 138–61) prohibited certain modes of inhuman treatment of slaves by masters he justified his prohibition by the general interests of the master class; all might suffer from slave unrest, if the cruelty of a few masters was unchecked. Not only was the institution of slavery upheld throughout the Principate: the hierarchical structure of society was strengthened. 'Nothing', wrote the conventional younger Pliny under Trajan (AD 98–117), 'is more unfair than equality' (*Letters* IX, 5). In the second century a distinction was more sharply drawn in criminal law between free men of different ranks. For instance, if the penalty was death, the more 'honourable' (senators, Equites, members of local town councils) would be decapitated, others burned alive, thrown to the beasts or crucified. These 'humbler' people could also be tortured like slaves. The common citizens as well as the senators forfeited the liberty they had prized in the Republic, for the lower classes had no better guarantee against arbitrary ill-usage than the upper classes for political freedom of speech. Liberty in every form was subject to progressive attrition. Politically, it was destroyed first in the centre, then in the municipalities, where the local oligarchies were more and more tightly controlled by the imperial government. Economically, it survived (except, of course, that as in all ages, the poor enjoyed it only in name, and the slaves not at all) until the fourth century, when almost all, like the peasants, were bound for life to the calling of their fathers. Even religious tolerance disappeared when first the pagan emperors, and then more markedly the Christian, required their subjects to practice only those cults of which they themselves approved.

In the Republic the discontents of the poor and the ambition of a few magnates had combined to produce anarchy, civil war and revolution. The outcome was political, not social or economic. Outside Rome, there was only so much amelioration in the condition of the masses as the maintenance of peace and order in itself assured. In the late empire, when evidence is again abundant, the gulf between rich and poor was at least as wide and deep as ever, misery and oppression as great. The cost of peace was high. To Mommsen Caesar was a hero; he, not Augustus, was the architect of the new monarchy, and his work was salutary, but only because in a society based on slavery 'it was the copestone logically necessary and the least of evils'. It demonstrated how the principle of absolutism would work itself out 'purely and freely . . . in the absence of all material extraneous complications.' Gibbon, to whose authority Mommsen appealed, had already remarked that an absolute ruler in the Europe of his own day could be restrained and modified by influences emanating from neighbouring states: 'but the empire of the Romans filled the world, and, when that empire fell into the hands of a single person, the world became a safe and dreary prison for his enemies'. In Mommsen's eyes the new system was from the first 'utterly withered and dead', because it failed to provide for 'free popular development'.[1] Certainly the loss of liberty was accompanied by stagnation in most of the arts and sciences; at the same time men sought consolation in manifold varieties of philosophy or religion for the wretchedness or nullity of life in this world. If there had been any spokesman for old popular sentiments in the Principate, he might not have seen much to change in the words with which Tacitus expressed senatorial resignation and bitterness: 'For twenty years (from 49 BC) there was conflict, no custom observed, no law; the worst crimes all unpunished, and honourable actions often fatal. At last . . . Caesar Augustus, safely dominant, . . . gave us laws to follow under peace and a prince. Thenceforth our bonds were tighter' (*Annals* III, 28).

[1] *History of Rome* (Everyman ed. IV, 439 f.), cf. Gibbon's *Decline and Fall*, ch. III, the last eight paragraphs.

Further Reading

THE *sources*, which the editorial plan has not permitted me to cite fully, are exhaustively cited, year by year, for dated events in T. R. S. Broughton, *The Magistrates of the Roman Republic* (New York, American Philological Association, two volumes, 1952). Selections of ancient evidence in translation will be found in N. Lewis and M. Reinhold, *Roman Civilization* (Harper Torchbooks, vol. 1, 1955), and in A. H. M. Jones, *History of Rome through the Fifth Century* (Harper Torchbooks, vol. 1, 1968); fuller and with more interpretation, for social and economic history is T. Frank, *Economic Survey of Ancient Rome*, vol. 1 (reprint, Paterson, Pageant Books Inc., 1959).

Of *general histories* of the Republic the most powerful and exciting, comprehending every aspect of Roman life, remains that by T. Mommsen (Everyman edition, four volumes); it is the work of a great imaginative historian, who had mastered all the evidence known a century ago; unfortunately the translation is heavy, and Mommsen seldom cited evidence. Rather more documentation can be found in the *Cambridge Ancient History*, vols. VII–X (1928–34); the chapters, by different hands, are of different merits. The full bibliographies are partly brought up-to-date for certain periods by E. Badian, 'From the Gracchi to Sulla' in *The Crisis of the Roman Republic* edited by R. Seager (Cambridge, Heffers, 1969), henceforth cited as '*The Crisis* . . .', and more selectively by H. H. Scullard in his *History of the Roman World 753–146 BC* (London, Methuen, 1960; New York, Barnes & Noble, 1961), the most up-to-date account in English, and in notes to *From the Gracchi to Nero* (London, University Paperbacks, 1963; New York, Barnes & Noble, 1964). I give below a brief selection of relevant works in English later than the *Cambridge Ancient History* for the period after *c.* 150. A. E. Astin, *Scipio Aemilianus* (Oxford, Clarendon Press, 1967) has perhaps the best account of the crisis of 133. E. Badian, *Foreign Clientelae, 264–70 BC* (Oxford, Clarendon Press, 1958; New York, Oxford University Press, 1958) and

SOCIAL CONFLICTS IN ROMAN REPUBLIC

Roman Imperialism in the Late Republic (Oxford, Basil Blackwell, 1969; New York, Barnes & Noble, 1968) are highly relevant, despite their titles, to domestic history. F. R. Cowell, *Cicero and the Roman Republic* (London, Pelican Books, 1964; Gloucester, Mass., Peter Smith; Baltimore, Md., Penguin Books), is particularly good on the background, R. E. Smith, *Cicero the Statesman* (Cambridge University Press, 1966) a well-written apologia. M. Gelzer, *Caesar, Politician and Statesman* (Oxford, Basil Blackwell, 1968; Cambridge, Mass., Harvard University Press, 1968) is now the fullest and most reliable account of all affairs in which Caesar was concerned, but see also the interesting sketch by J. P. V. D. Balsdon, *Julius Caesar and History* (London, Teach Yourself History, 1967; New York, Atheneum Press, 1967). R. Syme, *The Roman Revolution* (Oxford, Clarendon Press, 1939, and paperbound reprint; New York, Oxford University Press, paperback) gives incomparably the best account of the years 44 BC to AD 14.

The fundamental work on the *Roman constitution* remains Mommsen's *Römisches Staatsrecht*; the French translation, *Droit Public Romain* (eight volumes) is out of print. There is a lucid sketch in H. F. Jolowicz, *Historical Introduction to the Study of Roman Law* (Cambridge University Press, 1965). Of late more attention has been given to the *actual working of the system and its social basis*; M. Gelzer, *The Roman Nobility* (Oxford, Basil Blackwell, 1969), first published in 1912, was epoch-making. For a more comprehensive survey, see L. R. Taylor, *Party Politics in the Age of Caesar* (University of California Press, 1949; Gloucester, Mass., Peter Smith, 1962); important works of detail are her *Voting Districts of the Roman Republic* (American Academy at Rome, 1960) and *Roman Voting Assemblies* (University of Michigan Press, 1966). Other scholars have gone further in elaborating theories of more or less permanent factions among the nobility and depreciating the importance of issues; C. Wirszubski, *Libertas as a Political Idea at Rome* (Cambridge University Press, 1950) is a valuable corrective to the second tendency; against the first see my 'Amicitia in the Late Roman Republic' in *The Crisis . . .* and reviews of D. C. Earl's *Tiberius Gracchus* in *Gnomon* (1965), pp. 189–92, and of C. Meier's valuable *Res Publica Amissa* (in German) in *Journal of Roman Studies* (1968), pp. 229–32. A. W. Lintott, *Violence in Republican*

158

Rome (Oxford, Clarendon Press, 1968; New York, Oxford University Press, 1968) treats its subject well.

On the *army* R. E. Smith, *Service in the Post-Marian Roman Army* (Manchester University Press, 1958; New York, Barnes & Noble, 1958) corrects many common errors.

On *social and economic history*, besides Frank, see W. L. Westermann, *Slave Systems of Greek and Roman Antiquity* (Philadelphia, American Philosophical Association, 1955) with my review in *Journal of Roman Studies* (1958), pp. 164–70; J. A. Crook, *Law and Life in Rome* (London, Thames and Hudson, 1967; Ithaca, N.Y., Cornell University Press, 1967); S. M. Treggiari, *Roman Freedmen during the Late Republic* (Oxford, Clarendon Press, 1969); J. Carcopino, *Daily Life in Ancient Rome* (London, Routledge, 1941; New Haven, Conn., Yale University Press), based mainly on imperial evidence but partly relevant to the Republic. An older book, W. Heitland, *Agricola* (Cambridge University Press, 1921), is exhaustive on rural labour.

For Sallust, see D. C. Earl, *Political Thought of Sallust* (Amsterdam, Hakkert reprint, 1968; Chicago, Ill., Argonaut, Inc., 1961) and R. Syme, *Sallust* (Cambridge University Press, 1964; University of California Press, 1964).

Many statements in this book, some of which may appear controversial, rest on my other writings. Of these 'Italian Aims at the Time of the Social War' (*Journal of Roman Studies*, 1965, pp. 90–109), 'The Equites in the Late Republic' (*The Crisis . . .*) and 'The Roman Mob' (*Past and Present*, 1966, pp. 3–27) have titles that speak for themselves; for military recruitment and the persistence of the agrarian question in the first century see 'The Army and the Land in the Roman Revolution' (*Journal of Roman Studies*, 1962, pp. 69–86). My book, *Italian Manpower 225 BC–AD 14* (Oxford, Clarendon Press, 1971) deals among other things with census and population figures, numbers of soldiers, of military settlers, and of citizens abroad, and many aspects of the social and economic conditions in Italian regions.

Index

INDEX

B. Subjects

INDEX

aqueducts, 39, 58, 79, 128
artisans, 37, 96, 125, 128,
137, 153
assemblies at Rome, 1,
*8–11, 46 f., 51–4, 58, 61–
63, 65 f.,* 84, 94 f.; in
Italian towns, 9
assidui, 11, 13–15, 57, 77,
92
auctoritas, 46, 147
auspicium, 44

bakers, 128
ballot laws, 9, *65 f.,* 94,
110, 125
banking, 30, 38, 70
boni, 76, 93
booty, 15–17, 40, 105, 143
bribery, 63, 65, 101
brickmaking, 21
brigandage, 76, 117, 153
building trade, 30, 37,
128; see public works
butter, 33

canals, 25
capite censi, 13
censors, censorship, 45, 58,
62, 70 f.
census figures, 1 f., 4, 6,
18, 91, 107
centuries, 8 f., 46, 61 f.,
96, 132
cereals, see corn
cheese, 33
citizenship extended, 2 f.,
5 f., 9 f., 103, 105–7, 122
f.
clients, clientship, *47–50,*
54, 72, 79, 83, 106, 123,
131, 142
client states, 2
clothing, 14, 27, 33
collegia, 28 f., 127 f., 135,
137
colonies, *4 f., 31 f.,* 59, 63,
84 f., 89 f., *108, 144 f.,
150 f.*
conscription, *11–17,* 38,
64–6, 81, 85, 143, *150 f.,*
153
constitution, see Republic
consulship, 45, 50;
plebeians eligible, 47, 50,
55
corn, production in Italy,

22, 26 f., 33; imports, 20,
24–7, 30, 121, 138, 143
f., 152; distributions at
Rome, 30, 39, 63, 79,
85 f., 91, 94, *98,* 101, *109,
119 f.,* 128, *132, 135 f.,*
144, 152
courts, see jurisdiction
craftsmen, see artisans

debt problem, 17, 36, *50 f.,
55–7,* 63, 73, 90, 94, 103,
106, 126, *129 f.,* 142,
144, 151
democracy impossible at
Rome, *8 f.,* tendencies
towards, 51, 58, 61–3;
populares' attitude, 80,
84 f., 94 f., 120, 125
depopulation, 14, 77 f.
devastations, 32, 103, 115,
153
dictatorship, 45, 57, 67,
107
dock labour, 30 f., 79, 128
doles, see corn distributions

emigration, 37
Empire, its extent, 2
Equites, 17, *69–73,* 81, 83,
87–91, 95 f., 98, *100–2,*
104, *110 f., 119,* 124, *131,*
133, 140, *154 f.*
ergastula, 116
estates, size of, 14, 17, 19,
34–6, 78
exposure of infants, 18,
78, 136

factions, *68,* 77, 95, 140
factories, 20
famines, 20, 27, 119, 121,
137 f., 152 f.
farms, see estates,
peasantry
Fasti, 42
fides, 126
fires at Rome, 128 f., 152
floods, 20, 25; at Rome,
129, 152
food, 32
free labour, 36–8, 79, 99,
128–30
freedmen, *3,* 21, *37,* 58,
79, 91, 135 f.
fulling, 21

grain, see corn

hides, 33
housing, 28, 128, 149

imperium, 44 f., 54, 94
industry, 20 f., 29 f., 152
intercessio, 52, 55, 79 f.,
120
interest rates, 21, 56, 90,
103, 122
interrex, 44
inventions, 23

jurisdiction, 44 f., *48 f.,
53 f., 64 f.,* 72, *87–9,* 96
f., 100–2, *110, 118 f.,* 121

kidnapping, 116, 153

land, as investment, 34;
values, 14; distributions,
3 f., 11, 15, 32, 55 f.,
58, 64, 146, see also
agrarian legislation,
colonies; confiscations, 3
f., 32 f., 64, 107 f., 149
landowning, 21, 33–6, 70,
107 f.; estates, see
latifundia, peasants
latifundia, 17, 27, 34 f.
laws, 48–50, 53–5, 57
legates, 138
liberty, 44 f., 57, 93 f.,
110, 117, 125 f., 143, 153,
155 f.
luxury, 22, 75

manumissions, see
freedmen
Marxism, 127
meat, 26, 33
military service, see
assidui, conscription
milk, 33
mines, 30, 69, 71, 87
moneylending, 21, 70, 129,
see interest rates
municipalities in Italy,
9–11

'new men' at Rome, *10 f.,*
21, 50, 58, *67–9,* 72 f.,
76, 96 f., *154*
nexum, 51, 57, 129